No Son of Mine

NO SON OF MINE

a memoir

JONATHAN CORCORAN

Published by The University Press of Kentucky, scholarly publisher
for the Commonwealth, serving Bellarmine University, Berea College,
Centre College of Kentucky, Eastern Kentucky University, The Filson
Historical Society, Georgetown College, Kentucky Historical Society,
Kentucky State University, Morehead State University, Murray State
University, Northern Kentucky University, Spalding University,
Transylvania University, University of Kentucky, University of
Louisville, University of Pikeville, and Western Kentucky University.
All rights reserved.

Editorial and Sales Offices: The University Press of Kentucky
663 South Limestone Street, Lexington, Kentucky 40508-4008
www.kentuckypress.com

Library of Congress Cataloging-in-Publication Data

Names: Corcoran, Jonathan, author.
Title: No son of mine : a memoir / Jonathan Corcoran.
Description: Lexington, Kentucky : The University Press of Kentucky, 2024.
 | Series: Appalachian futures: Black, native, and queer voices
Identifiers: LCCN 2023051413 (print) | LCCN 2023051414 (ebook) |
 ISBN 9780813198514 (cloth) | ISBN 9780813198538 (adobe pdf) |
 ISBN 9780813198521 (epub)
Subjects: LCSH: Corcoran, Jonathan—Family. | Corcoran family. | Mothers
 and sons—United States—Biography. | Authors, American—21st
 century—Biography. | LCGFT: Autobiographies.
Classification: LCC PS3603.O73417 Z46 2024 (print) | LCC PS3603.O73417
 (ebook) | DDC 813/.6 [B]—dc23/eng/20231128
LC record available at https://lccn.loc.gov/2023051413
LC ebook record available at https://lccn.loc.gov/2023051414

This book is printed on acid-free paper meeting
the requirements of the American National Standard
for Permanence in Paper for Printed Library Materials.

Manufactured in the United States of America.

Member of the Association
of University Presses

To all the mothers—the ones who raised me, and especially those who saved me.

CONTENTS

CONTENTS

Part Three

FEBRUARY 2020

It's the before-times. I'm not yet teaching English Composition with a camera from my couch; my husband isn't yet conducting therapy sessions from the bedroom. These things will come soon enough, but for now, we're unbothered. We're taking a walk through our neighborhood in Brooklyn. It's February and we're trying to stay warm, and I keep making him stop to touch the fabric of my coat—it's a soft, brown wool that soaks up every last bit of the winter sun. Touch it, touch it, I say, and he obliges each time. We've been taking versions of this walk for the last fifteen years.

We walk and we chat and we point at the fancy apartments that we'll never afford. Though it feels like no time has passed, we've been out for a couple of miles and our legs grow tired, so we turn to go home. We find ourselves approaching the too-expensive Key Food on Seventh Avenue, and Sam, my husband, has the thought that he wants to buy some ingredients for dinner. We hate the place—the prices, the poor quality of the produce—but it's there and we're almost back to our apartment; why would we head two avenues over to save five bucks?

We huddle just off the avenue, near the loading dock of the grocery store. Sam is relaying his list of ingredients—orzo, hot peppers, mint, fennel—when my sister Jackie calls. She never calls. We speak once or twice a year.

I should take this, I tell him. It'll only be a minute and I'll meet him inside. Would he mind? And of course he doesn't care, because he does most of the shopping and the cooking, and I do the cleaning and the dishes. We've had a clear division of labor for the better part of a decade.

I lean against the brick wall of the store, between the loading dock and the fresh flower stall. Across the street is an old church. This is Park Slope, so adjacent to the loading dock is a row of well-preserved brownstones.

"Hello, sister," I say.

Jackie lives in a trailer just outside of the town where we both grew up, back in our mountainous corner of rural West Virginia. There's a creek that runs behind her trailer, like there's a creek behind our childhood home. The creek behind her trailer sometimes runs orange from acid mine runoff, and the one behind our old house turns cloudy when a neighbor drains their washing machine straight into the water.

What she says comes out so fast. She says, Hi, Mom's in the hospital, she's in the psych ward, locked up. Teresa, our other sister, drove her there.

"The psych ward? What is this about Teresa?"

She's speaking too quickly. I can't make any sense of it.

Hallucinations, she says. A breakdown. She's seen children in the closet. Your closet, Jackie says. Little boys from the neighborhood. Mom called Teresa at work and said, "Tell them to come out and stop playing tricks on me!"

Inside the grocery store, Sam is buying salad greens and orzo and little red peppers. Outside, I am holding a cell phone too firmly against my ear.

Jackie says, Mom called Teresa at work, and then Mom drove herself to the gambling parlor where Teresa worked, and Mom just kept insisting it was true, that the boys were there, and she wouldn't listen to anybody. Teresa had to get her boss to cover for her. She had to leave her job for the day, leave behind her customers who'd come to play video slots and keno. Her boss told her to go, that he'd been through something *similar*. When I first hear that word, *similar*, I can't understand what Jackie is trying to say to me, what Teresa's boss was implying.

I will understand soon enough. That same day, or maybe in a day or two, Jackie will get on the phone with the specialist.

Dementia, the doctor will tell her. Maybe Alzheimer's, but likely Lewy body dementia. The symptoms of Lewy body dementia can appear suddenly, often with a hallucination—visions of things that aren't really there—like little boys hiding in the closet of your only son's childhood bedroom. What I'll learn is that you can never really know what's going on with the brain, that things like dementia are nearly impossible to diagnose 100 percent accurately—not until the patient has died, until a skull is cut open.

I am shaking when Sam comes out with provisions for our dinner, though a part of me wants to laugh. My mother is locked up in the psych ward in the very same hospital where I was born. And after everything we've gone through, all the screaming and crying and cursing, the years-long silences—apology after apology for the *devil* inside her—where does she go, what does she see? Little boys hiding in closets.

MARCH 2020

We're taking a walk to Greenwood Cemetery. The month is now March, and this is my answer to the buzzing chaos. In fact, taking walks is about the only thing that reminds me that my body is still affected by gravity, that I'm not going to float off into the sky.

The walk from our apartment to the entrance gates of Greenwood takes about forty-five minutes. This is the furthest we've walked since it happened. The *we* is my husband and myself, Sam and me. What happened—the *it*—is debatable. That's what we're talking about on this walk, what we've been talking about nonstop for a month straight, and really, what we've been talking about for the entirety of our relationship, when fifteen years ago my mother uttered a phrase that changed my life.

What we're talking about is her dementia, of course, but the line goes backward and forward. What we're talking about happened fifteen years ago, and what we're talking about is happening now. What we're talking about is her body and her mind, is a cascading series of events that, remarkably, considering the time in which we live, has almost nothing to do with Covid. But Covid is, of course, another thing that we're talking about on this walk. It's here, in New York. We know almost nothing about it. We have no treatments. The hospitals are overflowing, there are trucks full of refrigerated bodies lining nearby blocks, and I spend my days—when I'm not walking—counting ambulance sirens. Six minutes, I decide. There's a siren every six minutes.

We're walking to Greenwood Cemetery to find gravity and, though I haven't admitted this yet, to find silence. Greenwood, with its 600,000 bodies, is the quietest place I've found in the city.

I'm digging my fingers into Sam's arms. It's like when we fly. I can't get over my fear that every bump of turbulence is *the one,* no matter how many statistics I read, no matter how faithfully I do what the behavioral psychologists say, which is, of all things, to firmly press one's rear into the airplane seat. Pretend you're in a car, they say. Feel the bumps. So I make sure that Sam and I sit together when we fly, because my fears haven't yet overridden my desire to travel. I shove my rear into the narrow seat, and I dig my fingers so hard into Sam's skin that he spends all of our vacations with bruised biceps.

We arrive at the cemetery, and we tilt our heads up to spot the parakeets. It's an unusual sight—a colony of bright, tropical green birds here in the middle of Brooklyn, the twigs of their enormous, communal nest spilling from every odd window of the arched, gothic towers of the cemetery entrance. Monk parakeets. Hundreds, maybe thousands of them. Some people claim they originated from a broken crate at JFK airport. Others say they were merely pets released to the wild.

I say to Sam, "Do you remember the Bernstein concert?"

And he says, "Of course."

It was 2018, two years earlier. We'd walked into the cemetery— through the arches, past the squawking parakeets—and there was a youth orchestra playing the score to *West Side Story.*

We'd sat down on the lawn then, and I'd become transfixed by the jerkiness of the rhythms—how alive Bernstein seemed to me, even with the syncopation of the timpani beats and the horn blows echoing off the two-hundred-year-old mausoleums, even as I glanced at a backdrop of a thousand, thousand tombstones—including one, somewhere just out of sight, engraved with his name. It was his birthday celebration. He would have been 100.

Today the cemetery is quiet. This is what I'm looking for, an escape from the death and dying outside—the ambulance sirens, the bodies in the trucks, the newscasters who warn of apocalypse. Her.

When my mother was sent to the psych ward, they ran tests. They found other things, dangerous things that she had known about but ignored. The aneurysm in her stomach had gotten so large that it could just burst. The blocked arteries in her neck and leg would cause strokes. It was surgery or death, the doctor said. Maybe not tomorrow, he'd said, but these things will kill her. And so we convinced her, my sisters and I, through the fog clouding her mind, that surgery was what she needed.

And so here we are: she is recuperating at the hospital; the surgeries have gone well. But there's a new rub. The doctor says she can never live alone again. Jackie and I have been fighting over this point. Teresa, the oldest sibling, has stayed mostly neutral. What am I to say, 400 miles away in Brooklyn? Where have I been for the past fifteen years to suddenly assert my opinion? Jackie, the middle child, does not make these points, but they're implied. She needs proper care, I say. Jackie says it's cruel, the idea of putting her in a home with strangers. I'm not there, that place that was once my home, and I haven't been there for a long time. We argue, and Jackie wins. My mother will not go to a nursing home. She will live with Jackie in a trailer by the rusty-orange creek.

I'm walking through the cemetery with my husband, distracting myself with improbable parakeets and memories of Leonard Bernstein. We walk and talk and I squeeze Sam's arm, and I'm afraid that if I stop moving—if I stop too long to look at the tombstones, if I stop to ponder the decaying bodies underneath the grass—I'll have to admit the truth.

Her body is breaking down. Her mind is failing. Clogged arteries. Holes in her stomach. Holes in her brain. What could have been, that's over. What we are now—that's as good as it's going to get. It might even get worse. The time to work on our relationship is nearing the end, I want to say, but in reality the time to work on our relationship is up.

We have to keep moving.

We come home from our walk, and I release Sam's arm. I don't check his skin for bruises. We are tired, out of breath. Our building is on a busy corner of Flatbush Avenue. It sits on a triangular lot, like a miniature Brooklyn Flatiron. We march up the four flights of stairs to our apartment. Our windows face south across a small, triangular courtyard. We have a view of painted white bricks.

There are two great things about the little apartment—the first is the cheap rent, and the second is that despite the brick-wall view, the windows face south and we're on the top floor, which means the apartment is surprisingly bright—so bright that I've kept alive a calamondin orange tree, a stick of a thing that has nonetheless fruited a handful of tiny oranges. An orange tree in Brooklyn! I tell anyone who will listen.

We're sitting on the couch, and my mind is racing. The ambulances are whirring down Vanderbilt, down Flatbush. I'm afraid to read the news, but I do so anyway. My mother is in a hospital bed recovering from surgery. One day she's there, and one day she doesn't even know the day of the week. I'm looking for the right word—is her memory fragile? Is it already broken? The doctor says these things can progress in days or decades. He doesn't specify what he means by *things*.

I wonder if she remembers what we've been through: if she remembers when it first happened, if she remembers all the years we spent in silence. I count the breaks, the years when I no longer had a mother. Her golden child afflicted with *that thing*—she could barely say it. She had to spit to get the word out of her mouth.

How many years did she cry alone in the darkness?

There's a danger to sitting on the couch during times like these. I'm floating, floating away, back there to what it felt like. To be a boy, a young man, suddenly alone. To be cast out of the lives of the ones I loved. And I recognize this fact is important, this word in particular—that if I were the one with holes growing inside my head, I'd need to remember that there was love—there was always so much love. For the first twenty years, I was her golden child, and she was my mother, and that all this happened *in spite of* love.

I count the years of silence. I close my eyes. I see the holes in her gray matter—the dementia creeping forward.

NO SON OF MINE

Ambulances whir. A plague descends.

I'd always known what would happen, and yet I'd almost willed her to say it.

I'm on the couch. I search frantically for Sam, but he's right there, in the bedroom.

I call for him to come sit with me. I pat the couch cushion. I beckon.

I need you, I don't say.

I run a hand through his thick, dark hair, my fingers forcing the worry lines on his forehead to appear.

There it is again—the gravity I need.

We've only been home for a few hours. My body starts aching first. Sam's begins to ache only minutes later. We pace the floor, afraid to admit what's happening. We wake in the middle of the night burning with the first signs of fever. My skin is on fire. My bones are screaming, as if they're being ground through the wheel of a mill. We have pinching headaches. Sam loses his smell and taste. I'll lose mine a few days later.

Sam has a cough, and before long, we can barely walk the short space from our bed to the bathroom. The news says the city's hospitals are far, far beyond capacity, to only come in an extreme emergency. Elective procedures have been canceled. There are no beds. There is no room left in the morgue. There are bodies in freezer trucks just down the block. There are hardly any Covid tests, and certainly none for us. No one knows exactly how the disease progresses. Our family doctor sees us by video, our drooping faces against the off-white walls of our rental. She says to monitor our symptoms, to take painkillers, vitamin C, and zinc.

There are no painkillers left on Amazon or at the local pharmacies. We aren't allowed to leave our apartment; we can't risk infecting anyone. We have enough acetaminophen for eight days. We hope that will be enough. We know almost nothing about this disease. Our bodies are burning, and we hope that we won't die.

On Saturday, one day into our illness, Teresa texts me to tell me that our mother has recovered enough from her surgery to be sent home, a word that now means Jackie's trailer. On the morning of Monday, March 31, 2020, on the fourth day of our illness, after so much sweating and writhing, we wake, and it seems we might be turning a corner. I am sitting upright on the couch when Teresa calls me to tell me that our mother has died sometime in the middle of the night. Teresa says she is on her way to Jackie's trailer to see the body. What I hear is that Jackie saw her and started to scream. What I hear is that when Jackie calmed down, she noticed that our mother was sitting in a chair with her eyes tilted up toward the ceiling. She was in heaven with Dad now, Jackie or Teresa or both of them will tell me.

Jackie will tell me that she threw out the chair, that she couldn't stand to look at it, that she couldn't imagine sitting in it ever again.

Here is what I feel that morning: I am not, in fact, better. The news of her death is like throwing gasoline onto my skin. My body is burning, inside and out. The sickness and her death burn me and pulverize me. Covid is a bone crusher; that's what I'll tell people.

I hang up the phone. There will be more phone conversations later, but I'll remember less of these. Sam and I remove our clothes and step naked and fevered into a lukewarm shower. We hold each other, and I am deadly serious when I speak to him. I say, "We can cry for twenty-four hours. After that, we have to put this away." I am afraid that my grief will spiral. I know that grief has a physical effect. We are on the cusp of recovery or relapse. This disease is novel, unpredictable. I have suffered enough. I have seen what this kind of sadness can do. I do not want to die.

I put to use the lessons I have learned from my turbulent relationship with my mother. I know that to survive, we must sometimes compartmentalize. We must set aside things to process later, when we have the health and distance. We must prioritize the things that keep us living and breathing. The danger in this is the risk of forgetting. But sometimes forgetting is not a danger at all.

We stand in our naked embrace in that tight shower with our skin on fire and the cool water pouring down over us. I hold Sam and look out the cracked bathroom window to the bright white bricks. As we hold each other, as the water pours from the showerhead, as the spring air blows through the window and rinses our skin, I say to Sam something that I have meant more than anything else I have ever said to him. I say, "I need you to live."

PART ONE

I

I could not sleep last night. I was closing my eyes, and I saw her face receding in rage at the hotel in Downtown Brooklyn, at the Port Authority Bus Terminal. How many times did we depart like that? This pattern began many years ago. I was only twenty. And then I was twenty-six. And then I was twenty-eight. And then one day, in the middle of a plague, I was thirty-five, and it was over.

The voice that keeps me up says, Be fair, Jon. Tell her story. Look back. And so I try. This I can say: With time, things sometimes change. What I see now is not her face full of rage. She is hurting. I can see her sadness in the wrinkles, in her distant eyes, in how she turns away from me as I kiss my Sam. She turns because she must. She does not, I think, turn because she wants to.

What I didn't see then were the tears she cried on the bus home. What I didn't see then were the nights she spent alone in her bedroom in the dark.

And another voice says: She saw everything and nothing. She chose to see nothing when she could have seen the thing you needed her to see.

I am her son, her blood, her genes. I sit up at night thinking of these connections. This writing stirs long-dormant feelings. My mother died, and for a year I went to sleep. I slept through a plague of all sorts. Now I am awake again. I am catching up on a year's worth of feelings. Now I am angry, and now I see her face again so clearly, and now I am disarmed, distraught.

The voice that keeps me up says that instead of holding a funeral, I am writing a book.

She has been dead for exactly one year and two months, and in that span, I am learning to exist both with and without her. She was living, and then she wasn't. No matter what anyone says, the finality of death is unnerving. I am her son, and, I realize, her mortality is my own. I grapple with what is left—the memories, the words, the synesthesia. What's left is her white hair and her nicotine fingers. I do not know how to balance all the pain she caused with all the pain she felt. I have to close my eyes. Like a villain in a horror movie, her face transfigures. Her face strobes too quickly—from smile to scowl to hate to terror. I shudder.

The voice says, mourn, Jon. And I ask, how do you mourn without a body? Without even her ashes in a jar? I was sick with Covid and my sister sprinkled her remnants into a tree—a kousa dogwood, which was a name I didn't know existed. I try to remember her clothes, her cigarette smell. I remember her messed-up teeth and that when she was at her best, how she couldn't contain her laugh and it would just explode out of her, knocking her false teeth straight out of her mouth. I try to locate these times and all the times when she was happy. It's jarring to see her like that—the times when she laughed without worry and all the times she cradled my head. The voice says, make her a whole person. Remember her old friends. Remember the photos taken at the bars. I am trying to grasp her, but I don't understand how to fix a person in time. I ask myself if this is what mourning feels like.

The pattern is becoming familiar. Since she died, I have mostly cried in the dark. I am neither morbid nor overly reserved. I am not prone to fits of hysteria. It's not that I wait for Sam to sleep so that I can leave the bedroom and cry, protected as if the dark is some powerful suit of armor. I cry at night because that is when I am able to remember her. Sam's waking presence keeps her ghost at bay. He is life. He is the day. I see her face in the dark, and she says, I cried every night that you were gone.

I will never not see her face at the Port Authority, as I pick her up, as I send her away—her body aging, her legs becoming more unstable with every departure, the devil inside her robbing her of the things she loves. And now a new face comes: I see her dementia-ridden in the rocking chair at my sister's trailer back in West Virginia. It is my mother, but the logical part of me knows that it also isn't. She says, I want to go home, and she looks right through me. This version of her, the one where dementia has eaten holes into her brain, is but a shell.

I want to say to all the faces: I was never gone. You were the one who left me.

Writing these words is like cutting open the skin on my stomach.

There is no pleasure in death.

Where do I start? Perhaps, here, on my twentieth birthday, the day that everything changed.

It was October of 2004. It was the long Columbus Day weekend, and we had Monday off at school. I had traveled with Sam from our college campus in Rhode Island to his hometown of Portland, Maine. We had been dating on and off for six months. We were staying at his childhood home, and I had met his parents. I had never been so far north. The whole trip felt momentous.

Everything felt new then. There was the gilded campus of Brown University, the obscene wealth of my Ivy League classmates, the rugged New England coastline. Every experience was an education. Every day seemed to open my eyes to a world of possibility. It wasn't that I had been entirely sheltered, but my home in West Virginia seemed such a small, protected place. I had spent a lifetime looking up at the peaks of the mountains, wondering what was on the other side. And there I was—crossing over into the unknown.

That trip was the first time that I would notice how different the skies were in Maine. The blue seemed bluer, deeper. It was like a postcard version of how a sky should look—strands of pale white light breaking across the ocean, that pale light against the washed-out clapboard of the sleepy houses. There was a dimness to Maine. It wasn't bleak or dark. The light seemed to tilt and gesture; little golden halos of light would appear and draw your attention to a window or a metal street sign. You'd catch the dawning sun reflecting off the glass door of a café, and the people coming in and out seemed almost enchanted.

And maybe on my first visit to Portland Sam too was feeling that nostalgia—he drove me in his car and pointed out his old high school, the restaurants he'd frequented, the beaches and woods where the kids went to drink beers in the summer. There was the famous lighthouse, and there the famous diner where lobstermen still gathered at four in the morning before the tourists came in. A picture of a boy emerged: I was learning about him and also about his world, so different from mine. And he was beginning to learn about me.

Portland is not particularly large, I now realize, but then I didn't have much with which to compare it. The population was some ten times that of my old hometown, but I could see the real expansiveness in the geography. In Portland, the ocean stretched out free and open from every odd vantage point; my town in West Virginia sat plumb in a tight valley, with the Allegheny Mountains rising up high on all sides. The sun set yellow to a sudden black in West Virginia. If we were cradled by the mountains, the Mainers seemed beckoned by the sea. I could see this difference between Sam and me.

His parents took me to a nice but casual dinner, and over conversation, I discovered they were ex-hippies of sorts. His father had attended Woodstock and the two of them had fled Brooklyn in the 1970s for the bucolic nature of Portland and Maine. Sam's father found success as a contractor, and his mother taught art and spent her days making wire and wooden sculptures of fish and birds. They spoke in a loud and lively Jewish Brooklynese. They were versed in books and culture. They displayed interesting art on the walls of their home. They had traveled extensively across the United States and internationally. They had a particular fondness for national parks, and in between the interesting art, there were framed photos of Sam and his sister in front of mountains, in fields, against the backdrop of the wild Alaskan coast.

Pause for a moment and let me help you feel the whiplash I was experiencing. I had spent the bulk of my life in a small town in West Virginia, grown up in a church of evangelical holy rollers, kept a big, big secret out of fear for my safety and well-being. See my wide-open eyes, then, as I take in Maine and Sam's family, watch me fiddle with my posture, control any vestiges of an Appalachian accent gone long into hibernation. Here is what I keep thinking but could not say aloud to Sam or anyone: They'd welcomed me, a young *man* dating their *son*, into their home. I'd been shell-shocked when they'd placed us in the attic suite of their old Victorian home, when I walked into the bathroom, and over the toilet was a crudely printed sign that looked like it had been typed up just for our arrival: "Don't flush condoms down the toilet."

(Sam will later clarify—the sign said "condoms or tampons.")

They asked questions, and I told them some of my story but edited out certain details. Small town, small house, blue collar, simple life. The unredacted version was that my father was a construction worker with a cheating and gambling problem, and my mother, who cleaned houses for a living, was so distraught and hopeless that she was beginning to develop a gambling problem of her own. My parents were in an unhappy and unhealthy marriage and in tens of thousands of dollars of credit card debt. My mother had resorted to a reverse mortgage to try to consolidate some of her bills. She believed that all this suffering was a test from God.

I did not tell Sam's parents that neither of my parents had attended college. I didn't tell them that to this day I still can't find a document or an alumni list indicating that my mother actually graduated high school, that I had stopped trusting what she stated as fact. I didn't mention that we had rarely left our town, let alone the state, that we had gone on a grand total of three vacations during my childhood, all three to the beaches of Virginia and North Carolina. I didn't say, as they told me how they owned a boat and spent much of their summer cruising Maine's coastline, that my mother's biggest dream was to get out of West Virginia, that her biggest love was the ocean, that she hoped to die listening to the sounds of the waves.

And it was often like that in my new milieu at college, with friends and their parents and our professors. I would spend much of my time disarming, making folks comfortable. Those friends and parents and professors would refer to my *quaint* house and my parents' *quaint* lives and our *quaint* existence and *oh wow! They must be so proud.* It was no one's fault, really, but I understood that the truth of my upbringing and the truth of my family back home was simply too much for most to digest.

It may have been during that weekend that Sam told me about how his parents found out that he was gay. He was in high school, and they'd found a link to a gay porn site on their family computer's browser history, a link that Sam had forgotten to erase. His mother had cried, he said, but not because she didn't approve. She worried about how the world would treat him. After a long, tearful talk, she and his father both reiterated that Sam was and always would be their son.

On the night of my birthday, Sam's parents had gone to bed upstairs and left us to our own devices downstairs. It was a big, old Victorian house with wide-planked wooden floors that had been painted blue and white in a diamond pattern. The floors creaked just a little when you walked across them. There was a kitchen with an antique stove and big front porch and a little stoop on the side. It was a cozy home, despite its size, that had clearly been full of love and many wonderful memories. We'd rented a DVD—some horror movie, if I remember correctly—and Sam had opened a bottle of wine to celebrate.

As we sat down on the couch in the den with our glass of wine and a blanket pulled over our laps, I was some combination of giddy and anxious. There was the sheer roundness of it—turning twenty, saying good-bye to your teenage years. There was the overwhelming newness—Sam's accepting parents, seeing how others could create a life and a family in such a different way than I'd known. And there was also the physicality of Sam himself, the warmth of his legs snug against mine on the couch, and the harder to define physicality of taking such a trip together, the pulse-attenuating quality of wondering if we would last, if he thought I was long-term relationship material.

I was waiting for her call.

That October trip was during my second year at college. For much of my time at college, I'd called her nearly daily. I would tell her about the friends I'd met, about the classes I'd taken, about how different everything was. I told her when I was overwhelmed, and I listened for signs that she was going to be okay without me, alone with my father. I missed her. I felt guilty for leaving her behind when I was entering this new phase of my life.

She didn't always say much, but she'd tell me that she was so proud of me, and her voice would crack, and she said she wished I'd gone to the state university, that I'd stayed closer to home. At home, the creek in the backyard still flowed—I could hear it when she took the cordless phone to the wooden back porch with the tin roof that thundered when it rained, where I could always see her perfectly, chatting with me while she looked out across the gurgling creek into our little slice of woods, up at the birds and the squirrels, at the occasional deer and black bear. Not much had changed since I'd gone. My father still went out on the town on a Friday night, she said, and my sisters—well, they were getting by just fine. If I didn't call her at least every few days, she'd call me to make sure everything was okay. She told me, "When I left you in Providence that summer day, I saw your face in the dorm window, and you looked so sad and lonely." She said, "I didn't want to leave you."

I'd told her that I was going with "my friend Sam" to Maine. She'd actually met him. I'd been living back at home during my first summer break. Sam and I had only met during the spring semester, but I'd fallen hard for him. He'd taken a summer research position far away, doing community health research at a tribe in Oklahoma (I got a job at my hometown newspaper). During that summer, I called him nearly every evening, scared that he'd find someone new and move on. But as the season drew to a close and his position ended, we were still together. He caught a flight to Pittsburgh, the nearest airport to my hometown but still a three-hour drive, and I'd dragged him into the heart of West Virginia and showed him off to my family as my good friend from college. She'd said then that he was a nice young man.

And how do you describe the kind of knowing that travels across hundreds of miles? The buzz in your gut that says something isn't right? I'm not spiritual enough to say that we were connected across state lines. But as Sam and I popped in the DVD and the evening turned to night, I knew she should have called. I had been waiting all day. It wasn't just my birthday, but my twentieth birthday. I kept going over the number, the symbolism. I thought for a moment maybe she was sad that I'd grown up, that I was no longer in any sense a child. She'd had a history of untreated depression. I was the youngest, her last. Fourteen years separated me and my oldest sister. When I did the math I realized that she'd been raising children and had at least one child under her roof for thirty-two years straight.

It was my birthday, and there was no question that I had inherited her stubbornness. I couldn't bring myself to call her. I waited and waited, and I said nothing to Sam, because here I was a guest in his lovely family's home. How could I complain? This kind of thinking would be the beginning of a pattern—the best and happiest moments of my life punctuated by my mother's cruel words, her curses both literal and figurative, her absence or, worse yet, her presence (even now, after her death, she hovers). My life would become a constant tug between hurting and marching forward.

And so I don't remember the movie we began to watch. I remember how dim the lights were in the house. I remember those blue and white painted floors (with the kids moved out, the house would be sold not too long after our visit). I remember that it was cold in Maine in October and that night came earlier than I expected. We couldn't have been more than a few scenes into the movie when my cell phone rang.

"I should take this," I said.

I grabbed my wine and snuck out the side door to where there was a small staircase down to the driveway, right next to the two-story garage where Sam had played poker and pool and sometimes smoked joints with his friends in the upstairs room. I answered the phone and began to pace the driveway.

"Mom!" I said. "I'm in Maine."

And then that buzz in my gut stopped buzzing, became weighted, sank me down. The giveaway was her breathing, the heavy static of the in and out.

"Mom?" I said.

And I could see her—in her favorite spot in the kitchen, at the table, smoking a cigarette in the dark. There would be an ashtray full of half-stubbed-out cigarette butts. It wasn't yet midnight. It was a Sunday evening. My father had gone to bed or was out at the bars. She didn't want him to hear this conversation.

"Mom?" I said.

I think I'd known it was coming. I'd known, somewhere deep inside, that she had to have understood. Somehow, some way. I'd known, and I was surprised that it hadn't happened earlier.

She broke the silence. "You're in Maine?" She sounded like a wolf.

"Yes," I said.

"With Sam . . ."

"Yes," I said.

"Your boyfriend Sam?"

Writing this now, my body still tenses up. With her words—this acknowledgment of a thing that had been hidden for twenty years—there was a great cracking. Everything I'd known that would one day happen was happening. I had tried to tell my friends in college that coming out was not an option. I had tried to explain to them how she would react, what would happen to me after. My friends would listen with kindness, but they could never seem to hide their incredulousness. *Would she really do that?*

I cannot remember the day or really even the weeks after that phone call, but I can feel that night—my body still knows that moment. I sit here typing and I feel both a great weight and then a great letting loose. If I close my eyes, I can picture the Maine night sky hovering over Sam's garage; I don't know why the detail matters, but I want to say the stars had to be out, that there were wisps of translucent clouds cutting across a waning crescent moon. I can feel the cold air on my skin. It was so much colder in Maine than in Rhode Island. And I can hear her still over the phone, her exact intonation.

She heaved and she growled. "Are you, are you," she said, stopping just short of the truth of it.

And if you want to picture it you should imagine this: The heart of a boy as he faces turning into a man. You should picture the moment his skin grew taut and how his eyes flew open. You should picture his posture as he stands in defiance in a strange driveway, in a strange town, and see how he stiffens and angles as if to battle. Feel him holding his breath, preparing to say something he has never uttered to anyone of his blood.

And then you can hear her snap:

"Are you gay?"

And the way I remember it is as if everything lifted all at once. The weight lifted from my shoulders, and a shell that had been protecting my fragile insides broke off and flew up into those stars. And the tears I cried came with words.

"So what if I am?" I said. "So what if I'm gay?"

And then we listened to each other's breathing for but one more moment, and then her breathing stopped, and then she said what she had to say.

"You are no longer my son."

And the phone clicked off, and I slumped into the pavement of that driveway, and I remember the cold Maine air, and I remember Sam running out the door and picking me up off the ground, and I remember crying and crying and crying after all those years of hiding. And I remember, for the first time that I had the thought: "I'm alone now," and I was not sure if that was a good or a bad thing, but a part of me also knew this other truth: that I was free.

I would find out that the giveaway had been a notebook. I spent my first summer break from college back in West Virginia. I was home from school, and I had purchased a black Moleskine and a set of pastels. I was not very artistic, but I liked the feel of my fingers smudging the pastels across the paper. Each night of that break I lay in my bed and called Sam on the phone. We were in the very early days of our relationship. We had met only weeks before the summer break began.

I was two things then: I was both drunk on young love and desperately lonely. I was feeling alive for the first time—in the beginnings of my first real relationship—and also stifled by a return to a hidden life that I no longer considered my own. I spent the first year of college living openly. In that summer home, in West Virginia, the vise tightened, and I returned to who I had been.

I missed him, and so each night I called him, and as we talked, I drew little pictures in that black notebook of him or us or whatever came to mind.

When I left to return to college, just a couple months before my mother made that decisive phone call, I apparently left the notebook behind. The story I've been told is that she stashed my things into the closet of my old bedroom. One day she had been lonely and missing me. She had gone into my old bedroom. She walked over to the closet and ran her hands over my belongings, over the little artifacts from each turn of my youth. She would see: trophies and shin guards from my time in soccer; a long, velvet robe from my four cherished years in madrigal choir; Legos; chintzy souvenirs from field trips to New York, New Orleans, the Bahamas; so, so many books piled high. There would be Math Field Day certificates and the collection of late '90s music videos my friend Krista and I had shot with a ten-pound VHS camcorder. Almost all of this, camcorder included, would still be in that closet when in March 2020, after her dementia diagnosis, my sisters and I would clean out her house in preparation for her move. My mother could never throw anything of mine away.

And so on that lonely day, as she leafed through my old report cards and glanced at the bookcase, perhaps wondered over all the novels I'd read, she stumbled onto the little black notebook. She would have leafed through the sketches. Gradually an understanding would begin to wash over her. Maybe the understanding had already been there. She'd stumble onto the damning evidence. There, somewhere in the center of the notebook, was a never-sent love letter to Sam. On the opposite page, she'd see a pastel drawing, all in shades of blue, of his naked body reposed.

I can recall bits of the letter—overblown, dramatic, earnest. And I can remember running my fingers over the pastel lines of the body I'd drawn, pressing and smearing the outline of his curves and the texture of his chest hair as if to bring him to life.

She found the drawing. I was no longer the son she thought she knew. Her deepest fears had been confirmed.

2

After my mother died and after our fevers broke, after it became clear that we weren't going to lose our breaths and end up on vents—oh, how that shorthand infiltrated—we were still stuck in that tiny apartment waiting for our doctor or the CDC or both to clear us to step outside. We had less than 400 square feet. A bedroom, a living room, a windowless hall of a kitchen. I found myself taking calls from the bathroom floor because it was often the brightest and quietest spot in the apartment.

We weren't sure if we were still infectious, and we lived in a building with more than forty units. I was so scared to subject anyone to what we had just gone through. There was this charming older woman who lived down the hall who always said hello and always called me Sugar. She wheeled a suitcase wherever she went and had long, black skirts and left her patchouli and sage scent wherever she passed. We'd by chance seen her marching in a sea-themed bikini in the Mermaid Parade on Coney Island. She must have been nearly sixty when we saw her in the parade, and I used to dream that maybe one day she would invite me over for tea and she'd become that kind of surrogate mother, that intergenerational friend that you always hear about in the news or see on television. I couldn't bear the thought of her getting sick, and so we stayed inside with the news of my mother's death, with our sun-deprived, disease-hammered bodies slumped across the couch and bed.

We videoed our doctor, and she said, you look better and I'm glad you're doing okay—if you're this far, you'll make it. She said she'd seen so much, in that way that implied everything while saying nothing. We all read the news, and we couldn't not hear the sirens. When things in New York would quiet down, when we were allowed to return for necessary in-person appointments, Sam's dental hygienist would ask, how are you doing? And he'd say fine. And she'd say that makes sense, that you'd either lost no one or the whole world. It was such a simple statement, but I came to understand that was how life usually worked. The grief always piled on. The hygienist talked about whole families—stop—just whole families, and you understood what she meant.

On the video the doctor gave us our orders: More water, more vitamins, a couple more days inside, and then we could go back into the world with masks. It was a ticket, but we still had to wait. We still had to stew with the unfinished—with the remnants of our sickness, the business of my mother, the blare of the ambulance sirens, and what seemed like a year's supply of bagels and pizza that friends had sent for both our sickness and for her death. The thing I wanted most was to breathe fresh air, and the next thing was to eat something that wasn't bread.

What we needed was functioning lungs, fresh air, to see the cherry blossoms at the Brooklyn Botanic Gardens.

Sam watched me stewing. He gave me that knowing look. I reminded him, "We will mourn her later."

Teresa called and said she'd been on the Internet and she'd seen this thing—she called it a system. *There's this system,* she kept saying, and suddenly I realized I didn't fully comprehend the meaning of the word. This *system* would combine Mom's ashes with a kousa dogwood sapling. Would I split the cost with her?

I had never heard of a kousa dogwood, and the idea of a so-called system seemed to me a gimmick. A kousa dogwood? Yes, she said, k-o-u-s-a, with its pretty little flowers. There were all kinds of trees, but that was the one that caught her eye.

Couldn't you just sprinkle mom's ashes on the ground of a newly planted dogwood, I wanted to ask. I googled the *system,* and the site showed a cardboard box with circular arrows indicating how my mother would return to the earth, how her burnt remains would integrate with the tree. You could pick the tree, but it was important to use their *system* to get the ashes in the ground.

Of course it was a gimmick, but my mother was dead, I was recovering from sickness, and all the hills had already been died on. I was stuck inside that apartment, and I had no idea what I would do with my mother's ashes if I were in charge. Of course, I said. And then I remembered the half-dead dogwood in our front yard back in West Virginia, and how when I was a child, my mother would always get depressed or angry at my father and then announce that she was chopping down another tree, and I'd beg her not to cut the tree and I'd cry and cry. What was left in the front yard was that half-dead dogwood and a series of stumps.

We had two days left in quarantine, and I told Sam that I was going to lose my mind if I didn't get out for even one minute. We were physically stuck, and that was quickly becoming a metaphor for everything. Sam grabbed me by the hand, handed me a scarf, and told me to follow him. We covered our faces in the scarves (the only masks we had—there was a mask shortage then, and the CDC had been advising against buying them). We ran up the stairwell, pushed through the door with the sign that said access was forbidden, and stepped onto the roof. It was a bright April day and warm enough to only wear my faux-leather jacket. I walked over to the edge and, because we had no street-facing windows, looked down Flatbush Avenue and saw for the first time in a week that the world outside of our apartment still existed. The streets were quieter than usual, but the world was still in motion.

There in the distance was the Downtown Brooklyn skyline. The new and the old: the elliptical Barclays Center and the art deco Williamsburgh Savings Bank Tower. The rows of brownstones and the dozens of new skyscrapers. Each year a new building would rise, taller than the last. They were topping off above a thousand feet now, the tallest rivaling those in Manhattan. Before we were sick, we had spent our weekends meandering between those brownstones and buildings, stopping at Brooklyn Bridge Park, watching the sun reflect off of the tidal flows of the East River and the gleaming edifices of Wall Street.

We stayed up there for a short but important half-hour, which was all the sun my pale-getting-paler face could handle after a week stuck inside. When we came back downstairs, Sam received a frightening text from our building manager instructing us to stay off of the roof—that access to the roof was, as we knew, as the sign said, forbidden. We had never received a text from him before, but there were cameras in the hallway, and he had apparently decided to start actively monitoring our movements.

"Give me your phone," I rattled. "How dare he watch us like that."

I imagined calling him and giving him a piece of my mind—I'd start with the poor conditions of the constantly leaking ceiling in our bedroom, of the fact that we were trapped inside during a pandemic, that we'd both just survived a novel sickness that had already killed thousands of our neighbors, that my goddamn mother had just died and we'd had so much unfinished business and there wouldn't be a fucking funeral and did he prefer that I break the window instead of letting the sun touch my face on the piece of shit rooftop?

Thankfully, Sam stopped me from calling him or saying any of that. As the blood in my face cooled, I realized that it was the first time since being sick, since my mother had died, that I had felt real anger. That it was the first time in that long, sheltered week, that I had felt much of anything other than sickness. That during the many, many years of the on-again, off-again messy relationship with my mother, that during each of my fights and breakups with her, I had so frequently looked at Sam or looked into the mirror and said, metaphorically or not, "You can grieve for twenty-four hours, but I need you to survive."

In the rising buildings of Downtown Brooklyn some see the destruction of an old way of life, and of course they are right; but when I look at them, I also see the possibility of renewal.

I had survived. And I was beginning to realize that there is a point when a body becomes too tired to preserve the status quo. There is a point when the old has to be razed to make way for the new.

By accident, the kousa dogwood sapling was sent to our apartment and not to my sister's trailer. The seller apologized—they had mixed up the billing and shipping address. It was sitting down there in our lobby, next to the row of fifty silver mailboxes.

I asked Sam to throw it away. I didn't care if it was living. I didn't want to touch it.

The seller said he didn't know what happened. He said they never made mistakes like that.

My sister called me when a new tree arrived at her trailer in West Virginia, at the correct address. She said the tree was planted. She had put the ashes in with the tree. Gimmick or not, the physical part of my mother had been laid to rest.

It is one year later, and I will get there, I tell myself. I'll see the tree and the ashes and the dirt. And so I circle and circle the rings of our lives, of what brought us together and apart, our roots and our branches. I will get there, I say. As best as I can, in my own way, I too will put her in the ground.

3

In the late summer of 2003, my mother dropped me off for college at Brown. She said that when she'd dropped me off, she'd seen me looking out that dorm window with a face so sad that it broke her heart. She said she wanted to go up and grab me and take me back home. I was looking out into the parking lot, and I too saw her face in the car pulling away. I thought, she's going to be alone back there in West Virginia, in that house with my father. A part of me wanted to keep her in Providence, to help her start anew. We're mirrored, the two of us—in life and in death.

We *were* close, once. I have to remind myself that in between all the curses, between the memories so thick with pain, there was also room for a deep mother-son love. She used to tell the world it took her two births and a miscarriage before she could get to me. I was her third child. She was thirty-eight years old. Her doctor told her to abort me, that she was too old, that I was likely to have Down syndrome. She said she knew that I was always going to be her gift—and that's what Jonathan means, she said, God's greatest gift. She never thought for a second of getting rid of me.

And though there was plenty of strife during my childhood, we'd also built up a lot of love and understanding by the time I went to college. In those first weeks in Providence, I'd escape from the campus and wander down the hill to the streets of downtown. The buildings were so tall and so grand. I had to call her and let her know:

"Mom, everything is wonderful," I said. "I'm meeting so many new people. Right now, I'm walking through the streets, and the buildings—it's a real city, you wouldn't believe it."

She was back there in our tiny Elkins—3.43 square miles, 7,000 people—in that dim kitchen or on the bright back porch. She'd listen as I counted.

"Fifteen, sixteen, seventeen stories! This one's twenty-three, twenty-four, twenty-five stories! You could fit all of Elkins into one of these buildings."

I wanted her to see through my eyes. I wanted her to live my life. But even then, I was sensitive not to push too far. Even then, I was beginning to understand that our roles were shifting.

I think that was probably around the time that my mother began to omit details. It wasn't outright lying, but she began to have this thing where she didn't want me to see the whole picture, that she didn't want me to worry.

"We're all just fine back here," she'd say. "Nothing doing, nothing changed. You know this place. Nothing ever changes here."

I didn't think she was fine, but the last part was true. Nothing ever changed. She told me no details, but I knew. What happened was: Father went out, Father spent his paycheck on the poker machines. What happened was: A flood knocked out the power, and those waterlogged outlets never got fixed. What happened was: more floods, and Mother began to close off rooms and ignore the black mold. What happened was: Mother threw her hands up, snuck out in the evening, began to spend the little money my father saved from his paychecks on the same exact machines that he'd for so long worshiped. She had developed a certain taste.

And I'd say: "My professor read to me in Old English. You wouldn't believe it."

And I'd say: "There's an actual princess here. A real European princess."

And I'd say: "I took the ferry to Newport. The water was cold, but you would have loved it."

And then: "One day I'm going to buy you a beach house. Just you. It will be only yours. You can sit and do nothing all day. You can leave the rest of them behind."

Those skyscrapers seemed the tallest, the biggest objects in the whole world. There was a little park not far from the campus of Brown on the edge of the hillside overlooking downtown. Kids would go there and smoke pot, but I would walk over and sit on a bench completely sober and wait for the sunset while the lighted windows of the skyscrapers overtook the remaining daylight. There was the tallest one that everyone called the Superman Building with rectangular towers that narrowed toward the top, just like the one in the comics. There were the new, glassy developments along the waterfront, along the river that had once been paved over to make room for roads and later uncovered in a wave of urban renewal. And down by the mall was the Biltmore Hotel, with its iconic red sign and the penthouses that seemed like castles in the sky—and, indeed, the Biltmore had once been home to Providence's only royalty, the ex-mayor and con, Buddy Cianci.

Providence at night was orange. It was the streetlights or maybe it was the effect of all the factories churning out smoke, but it was a definite orange that cast the world in a comic-book noir. Two weeks into my freshman year I was sitting around with a group of friends in one of our dorm rooms and that orange light was filtering in through the windows. Those orange-hewn discussions always veered toward the personal. We'd save our deepest secrets, our strangest confessions for the orange hours. We were getting to know each other—the hobbies, the dreams, the drugs—and I said, "I'm gay," and no one blinked and that was it. I dropped it into the orange nighttime, and I never turned back.

I didn't cry in front of them. I'd told a half-dozen friends back in West Virginia, and I was lucky that I'd had at least a few friends there who hadn't cared. I'd found ways back home to squeeze out little bits of life in secret places and secret cars with secret boys. These little bits of life had kept me breathing. I'd come home back then and close my bedroom door and control my breathing and pray that my mother hadn't caught on. I'd look out my window into the West Virginia night—black sky against blacker mountains—and feel trapped. When I arrived at college, I promised myself that I was done with all of that. I knew my family would never accept me, but my family wasn't in Providence. Providence was a fresh start—orange tinted and electric.

So many of the kids I met at Brown didn't seem to care about Providence or skyscrapers or the downtown or the orange lights. Most of them barely left the college campus. I had this friend, from Nassau County on Long Island, and her parents were New York lawyers, and I would start going on and on about my trips down the hill, and I'd start spouting these ridiculous facts about the height of the buildings and the steel structure of buildings and how Providence had once been one of the top ten largest cities in the United States.

She'd respond, "Sure. I guess. But it's no New York."

As a sometimes lonely child, before my family could afford a computer or dial-up Internet, I'd armed myself with whatever knowledge the almanac could provide. I'd read about the world's cities and countries and exports and religions. The almanac's trade was numbers, but in the percentages and statistics, I came to see a picture of how the world worked. When I'd been accepted to Brown, I'd done a particularly deep dive on Providence and Rhode Island and New England. And so when my friend shrugged off my comments, I would feel defensive, as if I had some personal stake in Providence's right to be declared a metropolis. I would just keep going on and on. I'd talk about the birth of manufacturing and the silverware industry and costume jewelry and how Providence had placed its goods across half the country and really even the world. I'd be ready to spout statistics about the metropolitan area, about how Providence was one of the densest cities in the country. I could recite the populations and relative densities of all America's major cities and metropolitan areas.

I'd cite the number of people per square mile, and I'd say to her, "Come on. Of course it's not New York. But it's a city. It's a big city."

My friend wasn't rude. She wasn't trying to pick a fight. It just wasn't interesting to her. She'd seen too many big, impressive things to care about the cityscape of Providence, Rhode Island. "I don't know if I'd call it a city," she'd say, and that would be the end.

I came to learn another fact. In my class year, I was the only student from West Virginia. There were around 1,500 students in the class of 2007. There were more students from some developing countries than from West Virginia, and soon I began to see that the place I'd come from was truly foreign to most of my classmates. West Virginia, my little town, growing up working class and being part of an evangelical church—what I'd experienced was so far from the norm of my peers that I might as well have come from a different continent.

"You really can't just tell your parents?" a friend asked.

"No," I said. "I really can't. They'd never speak to me again."

"Is it possible that you're just afraid?"

I'd had this conversation with most of my close friends. They were well-meaning. They cared about me. And yet the more I talked to these new friends about my past, the more we sat in the dorm hallways on those hazy orange nights and the more I went into the tough details that people said they wanted to hear, the more I knew that I would have to be careful about disclosure. There were only so many times I could have the same conversation and maintain my sanity.

"What matters is that I'm here," I'd say. "What matters is that I'm living openly at Brown University, in Providence, in Rhode Island."

My mother would call and say, "Jon, don't you ever forget where you're from."

"How could I ever forget where I'm from?" I'd respond.

And then she'd cluck, and I'd hear her take a drag off her cigarette, and we'd move on to the weather, which was, in her words, always the same: cloudy, gray, cold, miserable. She was so fixated on the weather that she talked about it like a person, all the things this awful person had done to her.

I joined a campus initiative called BUAD, or Building Under-standing Across Differences. It was one of those diversity initia-tives that was meant to connect students across boundaries: racial, economic, religious, national. I started college in the fall of 2003. Brown was about to make national news for examining its ties to slavery, but the campus had yet to build out its first-generation and low-income student center.

BUAD claimed to aim for nuance. The leaders would raise topics for discussion, and we'd step forward or backward into a circle depending on whether or not our parents had attended college or if we'd ever been unsure if there'd be food on our dinner tables. I was always standing out on the edge—poor, gay, and publicly educated—with a handful of students of color or non-Christians or the other poor kids. The rich, private-school kids would shift uncontrollably and avert their eyes.

I still have friends from BUAD, though we largely stopped focusing on our differences and found the commonalities that brought us together. Most of the discussions from that time have receded into the abyss of memory. However, there's a small moment that always comes back to me. I can't remember what the workshop that day was about, but I was sitting in one of our small groups around a table trying to explain to my peers that if I were to come out to my family, I risked being disowned. And it was further com-plicated, I tried to say, because we didn't have any money to start with and I didn't have any financial support. I would be on my own. Where would I go during the summers? The holidays? What would happen to me in the case of an emergency? I needed to take safeguards. (And there I was talking myself out to the edge of the circle again.)

That discussion always made me feel so awful, as if I were the one at fault, as if I were the one who couldn't stumble onto a solution that would solve all my problems. There were other gays in the group, and of course they understood my situation to some extent, but most of the people I met at Brown came from the kinds of schools that had gay-straight alliances, came from families that would have joined PFLAG. I had spent so much time looking for anyone who would understand—*really understand*—what I risked. What I needed was validation, was to find someone who could help me put my very real conundrum into words that made sense.

It was after that conversation as we were leaving the meeting room that one of my group members pulled me aside. I didn't know her personally. She was a Muslim woman who wore the hijab. I'd only known a handful of Muslim people in my entire life. One had been my childhood doctor. None had ever been a close friend. I was probably awkward and uncomfortable around her, young and unsure of how to make sense of her headscarf.

She said to me, "I have a boyfriend that my parents don't know about. I come from a very traditional family. If they were to find out, I would be pulled out of college or maybe even worse."

She didn't tell me what "worse" would entail. I wanted to ask all kinds of questions and a part of me wanted to get her number and make her my friend in commiseration.

"What will you do?" I asked.

She said, "I don't know. I'm keeping our relationship a secret. I'm not sure we'll last."

We took each other in for a moment. What I remember about her is that she seemed so put together. She was well dressed and poised. She spoke matter-of-factly, as if she were the kind of person that had already run through every permutation, had simulated all possible outcomes. She did not have an answer, and yet her straightforwardness assured me that I too might find some semblance of normalcy.

I have a fuzzy recollection of her reaching to shake my hand, which strikes me as odd. It would have been an unusual reaction after such a conversation, and yet that is what I see her doing.

She said, "I wish you luck," and I may or may not have shaken her hand as I wished her the same.

Though we never spoke much after that, and though I never found out what happened with her boyfriend or her parents, though

I can't quite remember her face, I never forgot that moment. In that short conversation, she had made me understand that I wasn't alone.

When I arrived home for winter break after that first semester away, my head full of literature and history and dead languages, my mother told me yet again how the weather made her depressed. It was one of my first nights back. We were sitting at the kitchen table. I could see something start to buzz inside her when the sun went down. On went the lamp; out came the cigarettes, one after another. She was at least a pack a day. I too had picked up the habit then, and we sat there chitchatting in between puffs, letting the smoke fill the gaps in our conversation.

When the cigarettes could no longer dull her antsiness, we got in the car, her worn but dependable Dodge Stratus, and drove the town in circles.

"It's this place," she said, and though she didn't gesture, I understood that *this place* meant the house, meant the town, meant her life. "It's so gray. It's so wet. The air makes me sick."

We drove from the old Tygarts Valley Mall, which by then was not much more than a movie theater, to the newer Walmart. Those were the two poles, strip malls connected by a ten-minute drive down busy roads—the downtown left fallow in the middle, the storefronts closing year by year. We drove circle after circle—two loops, three loops. There were cars everywhere, hardly a body on the sidewalks.

"Why did you have to go so far away?" she said. She could never look me in the eye when she spoke like that.

I had to tread so delicately. On the one hand, there were things I needed to say to her; there were things I desperately needed her to understand—about herself, about me. On the other hand was this new thing that had started to develop when I left: this urge to protect her, to carry her; there was such a physicality to this desire, to pick her up, to hold her in my arms, to place her somewhere soft and bright and warm.

She'd finished a loop. She was driving back down the five-lane—that's what they called the road from Walmart to town. The fifth lane, in the middle of the highway, was the turning lane. In conversation with locals—the barber, the grocery store clerk, my Sunday school teacher—this detail always seemed to come up, always seemed to matter.

We were close to the turning point for home, and she said, "How about a pop?" We went to the drive-through of the McDonald's and ordered two diet sodas. She pulled around to the back lot—the one with the view of the Tygart Valley River and the flood-control gates, the concrete and metal structures that prevented the town from drowning. She and all the older folks I knew were always talking about the great flood of '85. I was just over a year old when it happened. She'd held me so tight, she'd told me, as she marched through waist-high water toward higher ground; how she'd been so scared as the creek had overflown and quickly covered the floors of our home, how she'd carried me up that hill, how she knew then that she would never, ever let me go.

The glass in the car steamed over, and she tuned the radio to the oldies station, the volume set to the decibel of a whisper. Her dyed hair appeared ghost white in the dimness. I rubbed the passenger window and looked up at the stars—I'd forgotten how clear the stars could be in West Virginia, even there in the middle of the town.

My father was home watching the news or out at the bars glued to his gambling machines, or worse, off fooling with one of his women. I couldn't keep track. These were things she mentioned in passing, a resigned, two-word aside: "Your father." That was what worried me most—the spark that I'd seen as a child increasingly seemed to be absent; if she had burned hot when I was young, at least the fire had said to me she was alive.

I felt paralyzed. She recognized a thing she hated, could name it, and yet wouldn't act. This had bothered me since I was young. How old had I been when I first asked my mother to just consider it—leaving him, leaving our home, moving somewhere to start fresh? I know it bothered my sister, Jackie, also. I can't even remember the teenage version of my sister without picturing her screaming at my mother, yelling that phrase that we all wished would come true: "Divorce him!" It was a rite of passage in our home—for the kids to grow up just enough to tell my mother that what was going on was not okay.

By Christmas, we must have already driven two dozen loops, had diet sodas from Hardee's, from McDonald's, from Wendy's, from Subway. By Christmas, I'd become so frustrated with my mother's immobility—her inaction, her insistence to see only the gloomy—that I was practically waging a propaganda war. I would say things like, "Look at me! Look at where I'm going!" And I'd say, "If I can make it out of here, anybody can!" And I'd say, "You can clean houses anywhere. You don't need much. A one-bedroom apartment isn't that expensive." I would tell my friends at school, "She's like a woman from another time." I wasn't yet telling people that she'd been abused; I'm not sure I'd admitted that to myself yet or even fully understood what that meant.

It always seemed easy to me. I could see her escape route so clearly. It was like this: Get up and go. Take the car and drive. Put in an application and start fresh. How many novels had been written with this boilerplate road map? How many women before her had driven off like Thelma and Louise (and even lived to tell the story)? She'd survived this long—surely she had the strength.

I wanted so badly for her to feel the liberation I was feeling. Rhode Island wasn't some utopia, but it gave me the chance to exist outside of the cycle that I and my mother and my whole family had been trapped in. That Christmas, it seemed like all I did was interrogate her. I would try to get her to think the unthinkable thoughts. I'd find any chance I could to insinuate these radical ideas into her mind. We'd go out at night, and we'd drink our diet sodas in the back lot of the McDonald's. She would listen, but then she'd just deflect. "Don't worry about me. I'm just happy you're home. I thank God every day that He keeps you safe. He has blessed my life with you."

That was where she'd always land. I wasn't yet brave enough to refute her vision of God. God had kept her children alive and fed and healthy. He'd given my oldest sister a child, my mother a grandson. God had asked her to take care of my father, to shepherd his children to safety. He'd sent me off to the Ivy League as a reward for her hard work. See? God tested her; God tried her. God never made it easy, and why should He? If she endured, her family would prosper. That's what she had done, and that's what she would keep doing. "God will reward me for my suffering," she said, with heaven in her eyes. "God has already rewarded me for my suffering."

By chance, my first group of friends at college were largely Jewish. I'd try to explain the religion I'd grown up in. We were Christians. *Nazarenes*. Evangelical. Our church believed that you needed to purify the soul, that you needed to pursue *entire sanctification*. This meant constant vigilance. This meant wailing at the altar, as the pastor touched your head and the churchgoers looked on as you confessed your sins. This meant raising your hand and testifying. This sometimes meant speaking in tongues. If you opened your heart to God, if you rid your body of the bad feelings, the bad thoughts, the Holy Spirit would transform you into the likeness of Jesus. But you could never stop once you started. If we backslid, we knew exactly where we'd end up.

I'd dove in deep as a child, giving church and God the same kind of dedication I would later give to my precious almanacs. I'd gone to Sunday school and then to Wednesday night youth group. I went to summer camp and joined a regional praise choir that toured all across the state. I'd gone to the tri-state youth conference and watched a thousand kids get dismissed from an auditorium so that the pastors on the stage could perform an exorcism on the teenage girl who was convulsing and screeching from the devil's possession. I'd known the Bible pretty much front and back. My paternal grandmother's last words to me before she died were, "I always thought you'd be a preacher."

A world away I would sit in the hallway of my freshman dorm, and I'd tell this gaggle of quasi- or nonreligious Jews all these stories that seemed so wild to them. Our conversations would go something like:

"And did you go to church every Sunday?"

"For a time. And Wednesdays, too."

"And they spoke in tongues?"

"Sometimes. Not often."

"And no one knew you were gay?"

"If I'd been gay, they would have told me I was going to hell. There were no exceptions."

"I don't think Jews believe in heaven or hell."

And to that, I may have said: "I wish I'd been born a Jew."

She sat toward the back. She didn't go every Sunday. She was quick to point out that this was his family's church, not hers. And yet she was the one who took me there—who put me in Sunday school, who handed me butterscotch candies to keep me from fidgeting during the long sermons. When I was young and small, I'd crawl under the aisles and grab my aunts' and my grandmother's ankles. My father joined on Easter and on Christmas. And those aunts and that grandmother doted on him, the baby of the family, as if he'd had perfect attendance.

The Nazarenes inhabited their own peculiar slice of religion. They were judgmental, certainly, but often quiet. They were not dancing Pentecostals. They weren't as loud as Southern Baptists. There were moments of fervor—the rare talking in tongues, the testimony from the pews—but in general, the Nazarenes delivered their brimstone more gently than some of their evangelical kin. There was a certain kind of insidiousness to this kind of a delivery, something stealthy and effective.

My mother didn't join the women's groups or the Bible studies, and she refused to pay dues. She told me over and over that God didn't charge a membership fee. Her relationship with God was personal. But she still went there, to that church that had come with marriage to my father; and in this way, like so many aspects of her life, she remained stubbornly on the outside.

The Nazarenes emphasized entire sanctification, and as a child, this scared me. We were constant sinners, we were told; we needed to spend every moment of our lives giving ourselves over to God. The part that scared me was that I knew it was true, that there were the in-between moments—sometimes minutes, sometimes hours, sometimes whole days—when my thoughts or even actions were no longer pure. I've been asked when I first knew that I was gay, and I tell people the seeds were always there—little thoughts in my five-, six-, seven-year-old mind. Little urges. Little ways of looking—at the other boys, at the world. And so, even in elementary school, I'd find myself grappling with these impurities, these things that, if I didn't catch them fast enough, if I didn't ask God for forgiveness in time, would keep me out of heaven. This was entire sanctification, and this was the gift that the Nazarene Church gave me—that if I died at the wrong moment, I'd spend the rest of eternity in hell. I'd spend the rest of eternity without her.

My mother spoke of God at home. She spoke of trials and tests. It was the only way she could make sense of her wretched childhood, of the lack of money, of my father's infidelities. She told her friends, and also us, her kids, that if she sinned, if she didn't take care of my father, if she didn't stay with him, then God would take away her children. Sometimes she replaced the phrase "take away" with "kill." That was the kind of God she believed in.

The more my mother spoke of God at home, of what He could and would do, and the more the pastor of our church spoke of entire sanctification, the more I began to understand the thoughts emerging in my brain were acts of the devil. I went on Sundays and Wednesdays and to church camp in the summer. The pastor said, "The wages of sin is death," and I'd stop going to the movie theater and I'd throw out all my CDs and comic books. I needed to do more and more to stop the thoughts, to prevent that ultimate punishment.

I can see my old church, with its twin aisles, a hundred people crammed into the pews on a Sunday, fanning their faces with the paper programs. Sunday school in the basement has ended. I'm sitting upstairs with her. A few rows up are my relatives—aunts, uncles, my grandmother—all from my father's side. The carpet is seafoam green.

In this memory I'm no more than nine years old. The other kids from Sunday school sit scattered across the room, making faces at each other. But not me. Not today. There are greetings, prayers, Bible verses read. And then, the main act: My eyes are glued on the pastor. He's a big man, and sweat drips down his face as he rails again and again—those wages of sin, the fire of hell. My spine is erect, my body unmoving, as he goes on like this—the ups and downs, the lilts, shouts, the loud exhales—for half an hour.

I'm in a trance. My heart is beating at the pace of his words. Then somewhere in this pulsing memory he brings his sermon toward a close: he makes a gesture, and the organist starts to pipe— the first notes slow, droning. His final questions are, "Do you need forgiveness? Do you need to be washed in the blood of the lamb?" I feel like I'm having a heart attack. And then the organist picks up the pace, and the choir starts singing "Just as I Am," the verses and then that same chorus, over and over.

"Do you need forgiveness? Do you need to be washed in the blood of the lamb?"

He doesn't repeat himself, but in my head, that's what I hear. It's a trick I'll learn later in life. A journalism professor will tell me that if you ask a question, wait as long as it takes. It's a rookie mistake to try to fill the silence, to rephrase the question. Get comfortable with the awkwardness and wait, she'll tell me. That's when the truth comes out. People just spill their guts.

And that day, as the choir sings those same words—"Oh lamb of God, I come, I come"—I know the truth, that the pastor is waiting for me, that Jesus is waiting for me, that my skin is transparent and that my sins are clear for all to see.

Five minutes of singing pass, and no one answers the call. I can't take the pressure. I stand, tears streaming down my cheeks; I've never done this before. A hundred eyes all turn to watch me, my nine-year-old body walking down the carpet, slowly, nervously. I kneel down at the wooden altar, and the pastor shouts, "Yes, yes!" and then he leans over, puts a hand on my back, and whispers: "What is it that you need to say to God?"

And I wail then—the altar and my nose and my shirt are wet with my guilt. "I've turned away from Him," I say, so elliptically. "I've turned away from God."

There are murmurs from the audience, the praising of Jesus. As I continue to wail, as the pastor prays for God to purge the sins from my mortal body, an older woman answers the call and takes her spot beside me. People in the front row stand up and join the pastor, and they lay their hands on the other woman, on me.

"You're in His arms now," someone says.

When I go home my mother will tell me how proud she is of me, how she is so happy that I want Him in my life. My father will speak to my aunts and uncles and my grandmother, and they'll tell him what they saw. And I'll hear it over and over, "Oh, Jonathan. Our Jonathan. God loves you. We love you so much."

And for a while, I'll have my fix. And I'll look to the sky and know that I've managed to put it all away. When I die, I'll be there in heaven. I'll be there with her.

When I returned to campus after that first December break, there were days when I'd be a little homesick and think about my mother. I'd spend those days googling and reading all about West Virginia, trying to find some little piece of information that would remind me of what I'd left behind. One day I stumbled onto a surprising set of statistics. Elkins, where I'd grown up, was ranked one of the top ten cloudiest cities in the country. And another top ten: Elkins was one of the most precipitous places. You'd have to travel to Juneau, Alaska, to find a place less sunny than Elkins. Seattle, so notoriously cloudy and rainy, didn't come close to cracking either top ten.

I called my mother immediately. I read her the numbers I'd found. "You were right," I said.

She laughed. "Of course I was right," she said. "There's not a place on Earth as depressing as Elkins."

The complaints of my mother had always been so easy for me to dismiss. The more I read these statistics, the more I looked at the numbers and thought about what it meant to live, as one site said, 212 days per year under "heavy cloud," I wondered what else I had been missing. Her cold and gray world had always been a fact to her, even if my younger self thought she could magically make the sun and warmth appear.

And so I grappled then and so I grapple now with where to draw the line, how to make sense of the concept of agency versus fate, of how to balance bad luck and bad fortune with a refusal to make hard choices.

When she would later disown me and she would speak about God and tests and trials, I would understand that she had resigned control to something outside of herself. There was a part of me that could not blame her. The world in which she'd been born and then grown up in seemed set up to make her fail. If you had never been offered even the simplest kindness, how else could you make sense of such a cruel world than to see everything as a test from God?

With no money, no friendly faces to give her a lifeline, she would pray. She would pray for a change or a reward. When those never came, she would pray for her children to have success and to live the life she couldn't. When I would fail her spectacularly by being gay, she would at first curse God and would then beg Him for forgiveness. She understood from the stories in the Bible that trials were meant to be excruciating and that, ultimately, heaven was the only reward that mattered. I have more than a suspicion that at various points during her life, she prayed for death.

That first year at Brown was the first time I had experienced freedom. It was a freedom from the expectations that had been created for me. It was a freedom that was at times painful in that it required me to distance myself from the people I'd known and loved. It was a tepid freedom fraught with the vestiges of a dual identity, but it was freedom nonetheless.

I would have a few short flings over the course of that year. And by the end of the spring, I had worked up enough confidence in myself to ask a man out on a date. That man was Sam, who would eight years later become my husband.

I would reluctantly go home for the summer, taking a job as a newspaper reporter. I remember what must have been one of my first evenings back in West Virginia. It was a sunny, humid day, and I found my mother and father sitting on the back porch, her with an iced glass of Diet Coke, and both of them with dueling cigarettes.

I was telling them little bits about college and about my life in New England, and my father said, "I am very proud of you, son."

And my mother said, "Yes, me too. You've gone so far."

There was a silence. The three of us were staring out over the creek and into the woods, each of us apparently searching for something that we'd been missing.

My mother said, matter-of-factly, "I never should have married your father."

And my father shook his head and said, "No, no. She shouldn't have."

And my mother said, "He was never meant to be a family man."

And my father said, "No, I don't reckon I was."

They smoked a little more of their cigarettes or lit up another, and then my father spoke again: "Your mother will never be happy."

She didn't respond to him.

My mother watched the squirrels running back and forth across the clothesline, bickering and chattering. She said, "Don't make the same mistakes we did."

It might have been the best lesson she ever taught me. I took it to heart.

In less than a year from that conversation, I would be without a blood family. But I could say assuredly, I had made no mistakes in the process.

4

What does it mean to be disowned? For one, it means being cut off from everything that you have ever known: house, home, mother, father, sisters, nephew, niece, cousins, aunts, teachers, pets, possessions, *towns*. I was twenty years old, had spent eighteen of those in a small town in West Virginia. I suddenly found myself an exile in Providence, Rhode Island, the frigid New England winter fast approaching, among a group of people I'd known for little more than a year. Imagine: Twenty years of relationships, geographies, histories, all wiped clean.

In my dreams after being disowned, I saw green forests, running rivers, and beautiful, green-blue mountains. In my dreams, my mother would hold my hand while we sat on the front porch of my childhood home waiting for summer thunderstorms to roll in. But when the thunderstorms came, she was suddenly wielding a knife. And then she was aiming the knife at my chest. I dreamed for years that my mother was trying to murder me, in every way imaginable.

What does it mean to be disowned? By the time I had left college, it meant $20,000 in student loans and another $15,000 in credit card debt. I wasn't well off before my mother cut me off, a scholarship student in the extremely wealthy Ivy League. She was a cleaning lady, my father a stonemason. She never had much to give me in the first place, but I could always count on holiday care packages filled with an assortment of my favorite candies, $20 or $40 slipped between the folds of a card that never failed to read, "Miss you. Love, Mom."

Being disowned, if you're not careful, can create a pervasive sense of fatalism. Desperate for a semblance of normalcy, tired of telling my peers that I couldn't afford yet another fancy dinner or endless night of drinking, I took whatever money the creditors would give me and lived like a patrician. I could see three days down the road, at best. I lived in the moment, I suppose, but my mind kept going backward, replaying the events leading to the instant I became an orphan. I found ways to ease the pain—with nice meals and booze and clothes—and I didn't think about the consequences.

Being disowned, in the long term, has meant nightmares of my teeth falling out, and then, in real life, grinding my teeth down to the pulp. Stress. Anxiety. Depression. PTSD? My husband says I grind my teeth in my sleep so loud that he sometimes has to hit me to get me to stop. I've had thousands of dollars of dental work, and still, I have new cavities at every visit. Oh, and when you're disowned, and supporting yourself, you often decide that dental work is not really worth the cost. You let your ground-down teeth rot to the core and then cry about it when the cost of repair spirals into a sum nearly as large as the down payment on a house.

Being disowned means grieving over your loss—your lost family, your lost self. I gave up my religion. I gave up all religions. My husband, who was raised Jewish, explained to me the concept of sitting shiva for the deceased. He mentioned how certain Ultra-Orthodox Jews, the parents of children who marry outside of Judaism, or worse, parents of professed lesbians and gays, will disown their children and sit shiva as if that child is dead. This is apparently rare and rather extreme. But still, the phrase echoes: *You are dead to me.*

I was dead to my family. I was dead to myself. I was walking around like a ghost. I was trying, desperately, to be reborn.

As I sit here and try to find it, I have something to admit: There is no day after. What happened after my birthday in Maine, I could not say. After I collapsed on the driveway of Sam's old home, I know that he lifted me up or that I mustered the strength to stand. I know that I didn't stay in Maine forever, though in a moment like that, when everything you've ever known turns so quickly, it would have been easy, maybe soothing, to dissipate and sink into the frozen Maine ground, to sink down into the permafrost and to become the marker of a geological epoch, the era when mothers told their sons that there were certain lines that could not be crossed.

There was the expected peripheral damage, more lives disconnected over the airwaves. Teresa called and said she loved me, that she'd asked Mom to take a step back. Jackie said she was confused, that she didn't know what to do. She too loved me, she said, but it was also true that I was going to hell. I didn't care about Jackie's hell or Teresa's attempts at making peace. What they said never could have been enough. I resented them for being there, with her. *How could you, why didn't you*—I rearranged those phrases over and over when I thought of them. What I really needed my sisters to do was what she had done to me, which was too much to ask. And just like that, because I needed discrete sides to be chosen, I let them go or I sent them away or maybe we just fizzled. I lost them both for so many years.

I somehow came back to campus (by car? by train? by bus?), and during that year I had a shared dorm room with a kind man named Jed, but I mostly spent my days and nights at Sam's apartment. I say there is no day after because for that part of my life, time stops feeling linear. There's a blackness that descends, a deep, velvet curtain that lifts to show only glimpses of the weeks, months, and even years afterward.

Here's a peek:

I'm sitting at a cafeteria table with a few of my closest friends.

"Can we do anything for you?" one asks.

"No, no," I say, and I'm fighting tears, but the tears end up in my dinner.

Here's another:

I'm sitting in the financial aid office. I'm with the loan officer.

He says: "Unless you are legally divorced from your parents, I cannot reduce your family's expected contribution. But I wouldn't worry. They're only required to contribute a couple of thousand dollars. You can cover that in loans."

The professor says, "Of course I can grant you an extension. But I'll need a note from the dean."

The dean says: "You should consider taking some time off. What you've gone through sounds traumatic."

The bad therapist says, "You should quit smoking. You might find that solves your problems."

Sam says, "Breathe."

In the history professor's office I say, "I'm falling behind on work. I don't think I can get the second essay in on time. Would it be possible to have an extension?"

The professor teaches a course called European Women's History, an elective I tell people that I've taken entirely out of intellectual curiosity, but that I will one day admit has to do with a not-so-subconscious desire to understand my mother. In the course, the professor walks us through hundreds of years, through movements and vast swaths of countries and communities and shifting borders. She finds unexpected trends and the women figures who have been ignored or underappreciated.

This expert on European women through the ages looks at me in a friendly but stern way—posture perfect, back upright behind her wooden desk, her hands folded into a triangle just so.

"I'm having some serious family issues," I say. "I'm gay. My mother does not approve. I've been disowned and I'm having emotional problems."

It's an absurd thing to blurt out, but it's also the truth. If I don't speak fast enough—if I don't get it all out quickly—I'll end up a puddle. I've learned this the hard way. Every other day, it seems, I leave some closed-door meeting wet and messy.

Her smile shifts to a face of concern. Her eyes narrow just a bit behind her glasses. Her folded hands don't budge.

"Of course I can grant you an extension. But I'll need a note from the dean."

I don't begrudge her this formality. I nod and say thank you. I stand up awkwardly and promise to deliver the note shortly. In a future life, I'll understand this coolness as the mark of a professional, as someone who understands how to maintain boundaries, how to keep the floodgates in check. For now, I am grateful that I don't need to go into any more details, that I don't need to spill more of my guts into the room of a near-stranger. She may not know it, but she has offered me a kindness.

When I leave her office, I take a deep breath and wipe the moisture that lines my eyelids. Not a single tear shed; a success.

The meeting with the history professor necessitates meeting with one of the deans—a dean of something or such. There are dozens of them—the associate deans, the assistant deans, the vice deans, the dean deans—and I'm somehow directed via phone or email or both to the appropriate person who can write a tardy note for a disowned child.

I recognize the dean in question. I've seen her give speeches at schoolwide meetings or maybe my first-year orientation. She has that short, cropped, academic power cut, and she speaks with that warm, robotic voice that all administrators use. She could be gussying me up or berating me—in either case, she'd sound exactly the same.

"Tell me about your situation," she says like a well-educated customer service agent.

Unlike my meeting with the history professor, I quickly understand that this is a command performance. I need the note. My grade depends on it. I begin to spill my guts. I hit all the major points—gay, Christian, poor, disowned, scared, lost, confused, West Virginian. I tell her about my meeting with the financial aid officer, who says that no matter what I do, I am still responsible for my family contribution. And then I get to business.

"My history professor says I need to see you to get a note to excuse my late paper," I say.

"You know," she says, deep in thought. She pauses.

"You know," and this time she raises a finger, scrunches her eyes.

"You should consider taking some time off," she says. "What you've gone through sounds traumatic."

Of course she says this. It's the Brown way, the Brown student rite of passage. What she's suggesting is that I should take a semester or a year to go travel the world and find myself. In fact Sam, who was once not quite sure about his academic career, who was once feeling just a little lost, did just that. Before I met him, he took off to live with a host family in Ecuador, to learn Spanish, to travel the Amazon. Every odd person at Brown seems to have done something similar—it's Machu Picchu or the Himalayas or Florence. A gap year, a semester abroad, a semester off, a semester to teach sign language to chimpanzees.

I stare at her blankly.

"My parents disowned me," I say.

She blinks. "I know. I think that's why you could use some time to heal."

I wonder if she has been listening. I wonder if she has even looked at my file, if colleges even keep files on students like me. I wonder how to convince an administrator with a six-figure salary what being poor means.

"I have no money," I say. "I'm living off of loans and my work study. I have nowhere to go. I don't even know how I'm going to get through the semester."

"Maybe that's why you should take some time off," she says.

I am not studying Dante, but I know enough about him to decide that academia is surely one of the circles of hell.

"No, no," I say, and for once, I'm fighting back nearly uncontrollable anger instead of rainy eyes. "I don't think that's what I want. What I want is the note."

"Okay," she says, and she jots down a few scribbles on a piece of paper. "Are you going to be okay?"

"Yes, I'm going to be okay."

"Are you sure?"

"Yes."

"It's unfathomable what happened to you," she says. "If you need anything at all, you just let me know."

The word follows me everywhere I go. The dean says it's *unfathomable* what happened to me, and my friends say it's *unfathomable* that she would abandon me like that. The men in Providence drive down the street and scream "Faggot!" and everyone says it's *unfathomable* that strangers in tricked-out sports cars could stoop so low. I am growing what some would call a chip on my shoulder, but I find the more apt descriptor would be a grenade in my stomach. I explain, I explain, I explain, and I listen, I listen, I listen, I listen. The acid bile builds up, eats at the safety pin, and I know, one day I'm going to burst. I dream of throwing bricks at windshields.

Fathom, I want to scream to the dean, to the financial aid counselor, to the therapist that tells me quitting smoking would solve all my problems. Just fathom for once! Fathom that a mother would toss out her child. Fathom that not all humans have a safety net. Fathom that the poor people who sweep your floors send their kids to Brown University, and fathom that no matter what those poor kids do, they won't have what you have.

Years later my friend Mandy, the son of a janitor father and a call center agent mother, will find herself juggling student loans, New York City rent, and dental bills. She educates and works her way into a very good job and will still be treading water. She will tell me, "People who are born poor can never get ahead." It compounds, the poorness, the lack of education, the lack of a down payment, the lack of compassion.

I get accepted to the Ivy League, and I dream of being rich, of becoming a senator, of changing the world. When I walk through the Van Wickle Gates at Brown University, I convince myself that anything is possible. And then my mother says I am no longer her son. The professor says get a note. The therapist says quit smoking. The dean says to go find myself by traveling the world. My credit card bill stands at too-many-thousand dollars.

What I can fathom is two, three days, maybe a week ahead. I study and then I work a part-time job—ten, fifteen, twenty hours a week. I muddle on, navigating through the fog of trauma, the hyperreality of loss. I don't have the luxury of taking time off to find myself. I get As and Bs. I turn in papers late. I manage to stay alive.

I haven't always been so fond of West Virginia. I am painting with broad strokes, but it was a place at times that seemed limited, or rather, a place that seemed to limit. West Virginia seemed to trap people; the high peaks of the Alleghenies, while beautiful, hid the view of the elsewhere that lay beyond. For much of my life I yearned for that beyond—the cities, the people, and, like my mother's eternal want, the ocean. For some, it was traitorous to consider leaving. To express my desire to move on and out was to, in the process, declare myself better than or beyond. Among certain circles there was an expectation that one should make do. There was an expectation that one should aim only so high, that one should shorten his reach. Among other circles, there was an expectation that one should give back, to offer one's talents selflessly to the place that raised you. Maybe after so many years of extraction—the natural resources, the money, the people—this kind of talk was meant as a kind of tough love borne out of a desire to protect and preserve. Regardless, I at times resented parts of my upbringing, a resentment that was sometimes quiet and other times quite loud.

That all changed when my mother cast me aside and in the process forbade me from coming back to the place I called home. I was locked out. We did not talk, and my connection to what I had known, that line to back home, had been cut. After our estrangement, the term *home* had become dislocated from reality. Home, as I had known it, was beginning to lose meaning. Home, I realized, would exist only in my memory.

And so that is where I found it.

I would sit alone in my dorm room or in Sam's apartment. I'd let my mind glide back to what I could see. Picture a rolling mountain landscape—the gentle Appalachians, mind you, not the jagged Rockies. Let's not think of West Virginia in the wintertime, when the landscape is shades of white and gray. I liked to go there in the summer, when the green canopy of maples and poplars and sycamores stretches hundreds of miles, up and down along the contours of the mountains, the bright green deciduous trees along the floors of the valleys transitioning to the dark, sturdy evergreens at the tops of the ridges. When you are lonely, when you are alone, it's easy to filter your memory like that.

I took the same drive, over and over again, a once literal one that became a trip only in my mind. It was the drive into my town from the east, from Virginia, over the high peaks of the Eastern Continental Divide, where my car had struggled with the steep grade, through the heart of the Monongahela National Forest, where the rapids of Shavers Fork carve impossibly through Shavers Mountain. My father used to play a game where, coming down the mountain just a few miles from town, he'd pick his foot up off the pedal of his pickup truck and try to coast all the way back. I was a kid, and we might have been out swimming in the river, and I would be in my wet swimming trunks squealing and hollering and pounding on the dusty dashboard. We had made it once or twice to the city limits.

In West Virginia, the little towns are mere dots in the valleys—the houses seem to sit perched on borrowed time. West Virginia is all mountains and trees and rivers. I had swum in dozens of those rivers. In the summers, I'd pass the days jumping from rope swings, splashing deep and rising and then letting the current carry me halfway downstream. And my father had driven his truck up to the top of each of those ridges, and he'd let me climb up the boulders at a place called Bear Heaven and then up the metal fire tower where you could see all around for miles and miles, the trees and trees and more trees, and then we'd catch a rainbow or a golden trout and we'd throw it back in the water because I couldn't handle the gutting and, though he pretended to be annoyed, I don't think he cared that much for fishing.

All the things I had resented disappeared. I saw only the idyll. At Brown, I took fiddle lessons. I learned a dozen songs, and I'd play them over and over in my room and I'd cry. My teacher was a college friend I met, a brilliant musician who unexpectedly had ties to all the little folk festivals back where I'd grown up. I'd ask her for old-time tunes, the older the better. I wanted the sounds of the people who'd settled the mountains. And that's what I heard when I played—old men and women, sitting on porches in their small towns, up their hollows, along their creeks, wailing for a break, wailing for lost loves, wailing for the things that plucked at their hearts. My family never played the fiddle and they weren't much for old-timey ways, but when I'd been cut off from home, all I wanted was a heritage. And so I'd play the fiddle and I'd go to contra dances and I'd sit in quiet rooms and dream of the things that suddenly all seemed so beautiful, and I would sit there, an orphan at twenty years old, taking that same drive through the mountains over and over again, trying to invent a history.

Things that had felt inconsequential now seemed extraor-dinary. Our little house along the creek, the house that had once felt claustrophobic, that had been the site of so many fights and so much sadness, now seemed the very definition of quaint, a retreat on the water, with the gentle sound of the leaves blowing and the crackle of quick-moving water over the rocks. The town itself, just a collection of turn-of-the-century brick and block, a small grid of a downtown, now seemed the story of America, of prosperity. I could have written a book on the coal and timber and railroad barons who built the place. I read whatever I could find. I scanned over photos of the college campus, with its graceful mansions and classic proportions, all built by those millionaire barons. How they'd carved their tracks through the impenetrable stone. How they'd built an empire from the land that would power our cities and fuel our westward push. I even dreamed of the county court-house, with its textured stone facade; like all proper baronages, our town had a courthouse with that single, high-rising tower, our castle in the valley. I had come from *somewhere,* I wanted to say. It was a *real somewhere* that had mattered, and I was part of that lineage.

My friends at college would talk about New York and about
Boston and London and San Francisco and Miami and Park Avenue
co-ops and the Freedom Trail and the Revolutionary War and the
Pacific Ocean and South Beach and Saks Fifth Avenue and I'd say,
no, no, but did you have banjos and fiddles and the Civil War and
the tallest peaks in the Mid-Atlantic and the rivers and the creeks
and the runs and the fiddles and the banjos and Graceland Mansion
and Halliehurst and the trees and the railroad and the coal and the
trees and the trees and the square dancing and the mountains and
the trees—

I was manic and reaching and grabbing, one hand clawing to
hold onto the things I'd known and the other hammering in nails
to the scaffolding that would build this idealized world that I was
creating.

My friends were polite, or maybe I was convincing. They'd
say, wow, your home sounds so special; I hope you'll take us there
one day, and I'd say, yes, yes, that would be so nice, and I'd dream
about the day I'd return home and claim what had once been mine.

It's wrong to say that we never spoke. There was a period of months
where she was like my alarm clock. She would call me at 8 a.m.
I would be in bed with Sam, having some nightmare of her face
or some deep dream where I'd returned home and everything was
okay. I was never a morning person, and she'd wake me up, and
I'd be in a foolish panic, somehow each time thinking maybe today
she'd say she was sorry.

"Mom?" I'd say, half-awake.

Try to hear the longing in my voice. Try to understand what
it's like to be twenty years old, an exile in a strange world, as raw
as a peeled onion.

She'd say: "You're going to die of AIDS."

There was no preface.

Despite everything that had happened, there must have been
some part of me that believed she could change. And so I would
writhe. Sometimes I'd stay under the blankets, Sam half-awake,

clutching my arm. Sometimes I'd drop from the bed and lay my face and the phone against the cold, wooden floor.

I had no rebuttal. I just waited.

It was dying of AIDS or it was burning in hell or, more often than not, it was both.

She was a monster then, but like all monsters, she was vulnerable. Every tenth call she would slip up, she'd forget the script. She'd ask: "Who are you?" She'd ask: "What happened to you?" Her voice came through the phone like the sounds of a ghost.

And though I was raw, though I'd been stripped of dignity and stabbed with her vitriol, though her words salted my heart to the point where I thought it had shriveled to nothing, there was a little bit of something still pumping there; I had only ever wanted to thrive.

"I'm me," I'd say. "I'm the same Jon you gave birth to. I'm the same Jon you've always known."

I'd speak that tiny truth, and for a short time, that grounding thought was the only thing of which I was sure, though time would pass, and then I'd question even that.

We would listen to each other breathing, maybe crying. We would sit there for five or even ten minutes, and out of the static I'd render her tired body, her dyed hair, her face against the pillow. We were connected by airwaves and genetics and instinct. And then I would hear the phone click. For so long, she was the one who wielded the power. For so long, I continued to pick up the phone.

5

My mother is dead. My mother is dead and I am still half-sick in Brooklyn counting the ambulance sirens. I settle on six minutes. Every six minutes another one sounds. They whir down Flatbush, down Vanderbilt. I cannot say for sure that inside each ambulance another body is struggling to breathe, but in this age of crisis, it is more likely than not.

My mother has been dead for one day, now two days, three days, and the ambulances continue without pause. I do not need to read the news. The news is in the air. They sound at morning and at night, and they wake me up from all these dreams about death, about dying, about the dead.

I will see a friend from the neighborhood a year from now. We will joke about post-traumatic stress, about surviving, about helicopters. Then he will look me in the eyes and say, "If New York wants to recover from this, they should change the sound of the ambulance sirens."

But in April 2020: My mind says to forget her for now, to wait until my body can handle the prostration. My mind says to forget her, to compartmentalize as I have done a hundred times before. I am trying so hard, but I'm in a battle with the sounds.

The sirens trigger a memory, or rather, an amalgamation of many memories. It's not a fair comparison. This blaring sound has nothing to do with that blaring sound. This sound is not even consistent. There are three or four or more types of sirens wailing. There is the ambulance siren and the private Jewish ambulance siren and the fire-truck siren. And yet they all take me to the same place.

Elkins, West Virginia. Weese Street. Turning that corner. My breath picking up. It started when I was eight or nine or maybe even earlier—whenever it was that she'd let me walk alone to the city park or across the downtown to see my friends. The streets at home were quiet. The town was small, less than four square miles. An ambulance blaring could carry from one end to another, echoing off the mountain faces. How many times had I heard an ambulance and run?

I was eight or nine, and I would be running home from the park—not fully running, but nervous running, fast walking—the kind of speed your child self thinks will allow you to blend in. The ambulance siren blares, and last night was another bad Friday, and I expect to come home and find her dead, a gunshot to her temple or the rope strung around her neck or the pills foaming from her mouth. Again, I was only eight or nine. I might have been younger. I understood even then that she was hanging on with each puff of cigarette, with each cup of Lipton tea. He drove her mad.

The *he* is my father. The *he* could also be God. The one is linked to the other in her mind. God put her on this earth to take care of him. She said this over and over. God tested her. My father tested her. How could she separate the two? She persisted, somehow, with the cigarettes, with the tea, by staring out the kitchen window. This was her duty. I thought she would snap.

The test was money. The test was gambling. The test was a household in disrepair. Mostly the test was other women.

They fought like lions.

When I was eight years old, I would be swinging at the city park, and I would hear the sound of an ambulance, and I would make an excuse and leave my friends and run home, sweating through my t-shirt, fully expecting to find my mother dead on the kitchen floor. I ran so many times.

She never took her own life.

And yet, as I sit in Brooklyn, listening to the sounds of a plague that is carrying away the innocent, this is all I can think: she shouldn't have died so early. She shouldn't have died so alone.

My father had one rule. Friday nights were his. Until he was too feeble to leave the house, my father stood by this declaration.

Accordingly, for much of my youth, Friday nights meant sitting with my mother fretting. We would lie opposite on the couch and she would watch the Weather Channel or something forgettable on television, and sometimes she would ask me to rub her tired, calloused feet. The soles of her feet were hard like tree bark.

My father came home from work on Friday afternoons and immediately dumped his work clothes laden with dust and bits of concrete on the floor at the front door. He would trot from the front door to the bathroom and then take a shower. He'd leave the shower, put on a fresh pair of jeans, roll up the cuffs of a short-sleeved dress shirt, eat a fifteen-minute dinner—which my mother always prepared—and then he'd leave. He'd crank the engine of his pickup truck and then he would head to one bar or two bars or three bars or however many were in his rotation at the moment.

Before I was born, my father drank like an alcoholic (was an alcoholic?). I don't remember much of this. My sister Jackie tells the story of when she was a kid, of when her best friend was sleeping over for the night. My father came in at three in the morning and peed on my sister's friend, thinking this friend was the bathroom. Sometime after I was born, my mother gave him an ultimatum. She was always giving ultimatums, but somehow this one stuck. He gave up the drinking, but he kept the bars and the women and the gambling.

On Friday nights, my mother would sit and watch the clock ticking down toward midnight. She would watch the clock ticking toward close-time at 2 a.m. I would sit by her side and watch her watching the clock. Sometimes I would play a video game or fiddle with my Legos or read a book. Sometimes I would sleep. I was six, seven, eight, nine. Friday nights were my father's, and so this was what we did.

If he would come home at midnight, they would exchange words, and he would stomp past my mother to the bedroom, and the door would close and that was that. He was a muscular man, five foot seven, squat, with a body carved from training in the army—he had been a paratrooper in the 101st Airborne—and decades of laying heavy stone and bricks. When he walked on the thin wood floors of our house, the whole house shook. This, too, was a fight they frequently had—why he had to walk like that—but in the scheme of things, it was just a minor annoyance, a blip, compared to the big ones.

If he came at one or a little before closing, they might have a proper go at it. I would run to my room and peer through the keyhole or leave the door cracked just a little. I can only say that their voices were so loud that I thought the world might end, that the way she threw things across the room, I was sure he would strike back and hit her (though he never did). My sister Jackie is in some of these memories, like a protective blanket. When I was younger she would jump from the safety of her bedroom and snarl back as they went on and on.

"Stop it," she'd say. "He's just a kid."

She was the middle child, and the older she got, the more she would fight back as viciously as the adults. I can remember my father calling her a bitch. I can remember her words falling on deaf ears, or worse, fueling something that burned even hotter. And then one day she would stay out past midnight herself. And then one day she has graduated from high school and is gone from all these memories.

Sometimes my father did not come home at midnight or one or even two. My mother waited. She would pace and sit, sit and smoke, smoke and pace, from her spot on the couch to the table in the kitchen and sometimes to a chair on the front porch. Always, always, she left a trail of half-smoked cigarettes at all these spots. There were ashtrays with her butts in all corners of the house.

I would watch her, waiting for the cue. She seemed to rev up, to summon some hidden energy, despite the late hour, and despite the fact that she was always waking up at 4 a.m. and sitting alone in the kitchen, never quite getting enough sleep. It seems unfair to say that she seemed almost to salivate for this moment, but it's clear that the cycle that trapped her was not a healthy one.

She'd say, "Get in the car," and then I'd be half-asleep at 1:45 or 2 a.m. and running on adrenaline to keep pace with her. The car would be started up before I'd even closed the passenger door.

We did this dozens upon dozens of times. The waiting outside the bars, the sitting in the car; my mother chasing him, my mother fighting with the women in the streets of the downtown. These memories all blur together. Brenda becomes Mary becomes Janet. My mom is pulling Mary's hair, Janet's hair, what's left of his hair. There are back entrances to bars and front entrances to apartments. I was always in the car, the passenger window cracked; me, the silent, crying witness.

But there's this one night that's not like the others. Or rather it starts like those, but then something shifts.

We leave the house, and we take her old Pontiac to the corner by Gino's Pizzeria. In the parking lot, there's a statue of a goofy Italian man with a pet monkey on a chain. A decade or so later, I will read "A Good Man Is Hard to Find," and when Flannery O'Connor writes about Red Sammy's and the monkey on the chain, I will see the statue at Gino's and I will wonder just what Red Sammy has seen that makes him declare that title line.

It's two in the morning. There's Gino's on one corner (closed for the night), a convenience store across the street (open twenty-four hours), and the Starting Line bar just diagonal. The Starting Line is shutting down. There are patrons spilling from the front door. My father is not one of them.

They have both told me stories of the original incantation of the Starting Line—a place that changes names and owners every few years. It used to be called the Riverside, and the Riverside belonged to my father. He was a construction worker by day and a barman by night, but the story goes that he spent his own money on the gambling machines, that he lent his money to patrons, that it was, by all accounts, a rough but fun bar. Like so many moments in my father's life, he ran out of money and ran that bar to the ground.

The Starting Line is the third or fourth iteration of the Riverside—different bar, different owner, same story—and on most Friday nights my father will bounce from the Moose Club down the street to the Starting Line, which we are surveilling.

"Do you see him?" I ask. I'm trained in this art form. I find that my pulse quickens, that I feel this rising ball in my stomach that is waiting, waiting for him to step out. I am too young to understand this addiction, but I am feeling the effects.

"Wait," she says, her eyes locked on the bar. "Just you wait and watch."

I am her miniature, her sentry. I sit forward in my seat and look to the back entrance of the bar, in the alley, and then to the apartments across from the convenience store. Those are the apartments where the current girlfriend lives. I have seen my mother run from one place to the other—chasing my father and his girlfriend from the back entrance of the bar across the parking lot of the convenience store to the steps of the girlfriend's apartment. I have seen my mother shove him out of the way. I have seen my mother rip at the girlfriend's hair and pull her from the apartment steps into the middle of the street. I have cheered my mother on from my front-row seat in the car.

But tonight that does not happen. Tonight we wait until 2:30 a.m., and when the last lights of the bar have been turned off, when the bartender leaves and locks the front door, my father is nowhere to be found. My mother says nothing. She starts the car, and I dare not speak, and in a few moments, I am back home and put to bed in my room, sad that the night has resulted in nothing but this anticlimax. Before long I am asleep, and she closes my door.

I hear them at four or four-thirty. The house is small. I know where they are standing from the sound of their voices. He must have just come in the front door. She is blocking his path to their bedroom and is already screaming.

He has not often come home this late. And coming home this late means he has been into some kind of terrible trouble. The trouble would be better if he'd been locked up for a DUI, if he'd struck another telephone pole, if he'd passed out in a field. But the trouble, I hear from my mother's shouting, is the woman kind.

My mother screams. God, she can scream loudly. There is some litany of "Where have you been" and "What have you done" and "Leave" and "Never come back again."

My father says, "Woman, calm down."

She has done this before—many times. I have heard these same phrases, and I've seen her gather his flannel shirts and work jeans into black trash bags and toss them onto the sidewalk. And he has left many times before, for a day or two or sometimes three, and she will cry and then be lonely and then she will pick up the phone and dial the number where he is staying and she will ask me to ask him to come back home.

But there is something different in her voice tonight. There's a desperate crack that even my immature self can detect. And the crack is soon followed by the sound of glass breaking. She's thrown an ashtray against the wall. "Leave," she seethes, and when he doesn't, she finds some heavy object that I can't spy from the crack in the door, and she throws this against the mirror on the wall, breaking the mirror. "Leave!" she screams.

This goes on, and with each "Woman, calm down," she tosses something else, and before long, she is screaming and crying and chasing him with all the glass in the house until there is a trail of shards across the floor and he has run out the front door and started his truck and driven away.

When he is gone, I come out of my room, but she has snapped, it seems, whatever that means, but it's the phrase that comes to my childhood mind. She picks up a dining-room chair and throws it across the room, smashing the light fixture attached to the ceiling fan. Blue sparks fly from the fixture. She picks up another chair and smashes it against the wall. The wooden legs splinter and break. I am crying and pleading: "Mommy, please."

Those are the only words I can say, but I am following her around and retreating, like a scared mouse that has been caught and can't find an exit.

"Mommy, please."

And then she goes into the kitchen, and she finds the plates. And they're against the wall and across the tile floor. She is heaving and letting out guttural cries.

She goes for the coffee mugs, the tea cups, the drinking glasses. She clears the cabinets. She is barefoot and crunching across the broken glass looking for more. I am begging her to be careful, while I myself am tiptoeing across the wreckage of her marriage.

I don't know what she is looking for, but she leaves nothing untouched. The chairs, the dishware, the lamps, the overhead lights, the mirrors, the ashtrays, the ceramic angels—anything that can be destroyed. I see glass shards and wooden splinters and sometimes more sparks. When she takes out another ceiling light, I am scared we will be electrocuted or the house will burn down. There is blood on her fingers. There is blood on her feet.

And she wails as she goes. Scream, break, crunch. All the floors are covered—the living room, the dining room, the kitchen. There is nowhere to walk without stepping on it. She breaks the keepsakes. The nice furniture. She does not break the windows. For some reason, she doesn't break the china cabinet, which is probably the most expensive piece of furniture in our home.

She goes on until there is almost nothing left to break. She surveys the room. And then, when her mind can make no more sense, can't bear to think even one step further ahead, she collapses in a heap at the front door, in a pile of shards of glass.

She is breathing strangely. She is not responding to my voice or my touch.

I say, "Mommy, please don't die."

She is breathing heavily and looking off into some distance that I can't see, and there are tears dripping very slowly from the corners of her eyes. There is blood on the floor. I am sure she is dying. I latch onto her, can feel her heaving chest, and I say, "Mommy, I love you so much. Mommy, please don't die on me. I need you to live, Mommy. I need you to live for me."

I will not connect the dots for a long time. I will not understand what has happened to her, why her chest moved so quickly up and down.

One day, because I am her son, because she has declared me no longer her son, she will call me while I am sitting in my bedroom, and she will tell me that I am dying of AIDS, that I am going to hell, and I too will collapse onto the floor, and I too will find my chest heaving uncontrollably, and I too will be focused on something out there beyond the walls of my own home, something I will never quite be able to place, and I will hear a voice, this one coming from my Sam, and I will feel his strong hands on my shoulders, and he will hug me very tightly and shove a paper bag to my mouth, and he will say, "Breathe."

It took me a long time to learn how to love someone without hurting them, without hurting myself. I ask Sam if he remembers, and he does, of course, but only vaguely because we're different like that.

There was an incident that sounds so minor. We were in his apartment, maybe a year into our relationship. We were in some kind of stupid fight. I was jealous, possessive, and scared of being abandoned. Sam was all I had, and yet I worried constantly that I had trapped him, that he was afraid to leave me because I had been disowned. I was guilt-ridden.

It didn't matter what we were fighting about. What mattered was that I was vicious. I used to have such a hot temper. I'd go from smiling and laughing to boiling in just a second. It still happens, but rarely. I would scream, and his roommates were probably so frightened.

One day, we were sitting in his room, fighting over something that truly didn't matter. I found that my screaming didn't work—I had tried. I had pelted him with my yelling, had tried to get a rise out of him, had tried to make him scream back. But he wasn't like that. He would take whatever I was saying and put it in a place that I couldn't see. It created this situation where I could sit there for half an hour just yelling and yelling and threading my complaints, one after the other. And he'd take them all, and look at me or away, and he'd stash them in that hidden place.

And I hated it. I needed him to say something. I needed to have a reason to scream. I needed a surface to bounce my rage off of. But he wouldn't take part in any of it. He just sat there.

I picked up a pillow, and I let out a scream, and I threw it at his face. It was just a pillow, but it must have hit him hard, and I'd never, ever thrown anything before. He looked at me with the saddest eyes. He asked me why I'd done that, how I could do that.

And I think, then, it was the first time I'd seen myself objectively in quite some time, the first time I was beginning to understand just how much of what I'd learned had been dangerous, had been misguided.

It took me a while to become the kind of person that Sam deserved.

I apologized then, and years later, when I began to understand what had happened, I would tell him again that I was sorry, that "I was taught that love was violent, that you had to love violently if it was real."

I tried so hard to get my mother to unlearn that lesson, but she didn't want to hear it.

6

I am grappling with an issue of fairness. I am worried that I will go too far without giving my mother her chance to be heard. And what would that mean, anyway? I am puzzling over this problem, just as I've done for most of my conscious life. I don't think there's a day that's gone by since my twentieth birthday that I haven't spent trying to understand her, that I haven't tried to put her actions in context (and before that, even—when did this all begin?). What this means is that some part of my brain is perpetually trying to explain her actions, to find the root cause for them, and what this really comes dangerously close to is the notion that her actions have an excuse, that if I search hard and long enough the hurt and pain she caused me can be written away. *But she hurt more,* a voice says, and I don't doubt that. So here I am, operating the world's worst justice system from the recesses of my brain.

What do we owe our mothers? I suppose, at the very least, honesty. And maybe a chance to be heard.

Here are the facts: My mother was born in the postwar year of 1946 in Elkins, West Virginia, now a town of about 7,000. She was the eldest of six children and the only one of those children who did not share the same father. My mother was, for lack of a more euphemistic phrase, a bastard. This fact would directly harm her in her youth and would haunt her into the last years of her adulthood. Her own mother refused to tell her the name of her father. My grandmother would take this name to the grave. My mother's father was a blot, a stain, and was not to be spoken of. My mother would spend her life searching for the identity of this man. She believed that she had seen him when she was a young child (he was throwing pennies to her as she walked along the railroad tracks) and when she was a married woman (the strange man in the black coat who'd shown up at the door and asked to speak to Jack, my father, and then left when she said that Jack was not home).

My grandmother married another man soon after my mother's birth, and this man would father my mother's five half-siblings. My mother assumed her stepfather's surname, but from what she told me, it's clear that he never accepted her as his own. He was a wicked man, she said. She would tell me stories that scream of abuse, though she would never have used such words herself. The story I always remember involves his alcoholism. She paints him writhing on the floor on a day that all the booze in the house had run dry. She would tell the story from the vantage point of a staircase. She is a little girl, maybe seven, maybe eight. She is sitting on the staircase, watching him writhe, and he is watching her sitting on the stairs. He says, "Get the rubbing alcohol, you little bitch," and of course, she does as ordered.

The stories she told me of her childhood are conflicting and not entirely consistent. Dates and places change. Things don't always fit neatly on a timeline, but I don't think she ever lied to me about her past. What I remember of my own trauma is anything but clear and consistent. In the weeks and months after being disowned, I see mostly a fog but also sharp bolts of color—the haziness of everyday survival, and then the lightning-bright moments of both intense pain and ecstasy. I have at times gone down the rabbit hole to try to match up my memories with pieces of evidence. It's not easy for me to admit that the evidence—the plane tickets, the receipts, the photographs—doesn't always conform to my understanding of the past. Abuse and trauma surface at will, intrude on memories where they don't belong.

These are some of the things that my mother has told me: She spent summers or whole years being shipped off to live with aunts and uncles in small towns scattered across the state of West Virginia. I don't know why or how or whose choice this was, but she spoke fondly of these memories. She would say wonderful things about her aunts and uncles and the memories she made running around with kids who knew so little about her background, about the little things her aunts bought her as treats, about the way they combed her hair. These people, it seemed, touched her gently, treated her with dignity. I never heard her say a positive thing about the home she grew up in, about the man who would not accept her as his own.

And of that home and the people in it: She said that she was raised and told that her last name was that of her stepfather, only to learn that in fact the last name on her birth certificate was my grandmother's maiden name. She discovered this while trying to apply for a marriage certificate. "I was *not* a Manolidis," she would say. "I found out I was a Ware." She told me this, and yet when I look at documents, I see the contradictions. On my birth certificate, there she is: Patricia Ann Manolidis. On the marriage index from Maryland where she'd eloped: Patricia Ann Ware. I have gently probed her about this naming issue, about if her name was ever legally changed or if she just continued to write Manolidis out of habit. I asked her what I should say when a person or a form asks me for her maiden name, what name she thought of when she thought of herself. "I was a Manolidis," she said. "I was also a Ware." And, I suppose, to her, it did not matter anymore. After she married my father, she had become a Corcoran. So I pushed no further.

In her teens she either ran away or just plain announced that she was moving out of that abusive house. Which of those it was is fuzzy to me. Her stories would come to me in bits and pieces, and my attempts at clarification always resulted in half-answers, half-formed anecdotes. What I know is that she did leave. She moved in with a friend in her neighborhood and spent the last years of high school there, living under the care of her friend's parents. My mother tells me she graduated high school, but her name is conspicuously missing from the graduation lists posted on her high school alumni site. I have searched years forward and back, looking for some indication that she actually graduated. I see the names of my aunts and uncles and old neighbors, but my mother is not there.

I could call some of her brothers or her sister who are still living; they might have the answers to some of these questions. But these siblings were never much part of her life, nor were they part of mine. I am not sure I have ever met her only sister. In general, she left me with the sense that few in that house—not her mother, not her stepfather, and rarely her siblings—treated her as human. There are stories and examples of this, though she didn't like to talk about these moments very much. These little insights would come so casually and fleetingly. Her stepfather was a bad man (she'd flick her cigarette). Her mother never seemed to care (a sip of Diet Coke). I got the sense that what she felt about her family was more sadness than anger. But it was a kind of sadness that seared.

This is the memory I have of my grandmother: I am in middle school, and I've come down with some kind of sickness. My mother is working and unreachable. My father is working and unreachable. My Grandmother Teresa, my father's mother, is out of the house and unreachable. And so the secretary arrives at the last number on my emergency contact list: My Grandmother June. Grandmother June is told of my illness. She says she will be there shortly to pick me up.

I am sick and sitting in a chair in the main hallway outside the principal's office, not far from the entrance of the building. I am very likely anxious. In middle school, I would call out sick if the boys at recess had called me another name. I would call out sick if one of the cruel girls had made another innuendo. My mother usually didn't ask questions. She'd pet me and fix me lunch and put me to bed on the couch. As a child, I only very rarely went to visit my Grandmother June.

I am sitting, anxious and waiting. The drive from my grandmother's trailer park can't be more than ten minutes, but when you're that young and that nervous, time has a way of stretching. The clock ticks. There are myriad footsteps in the hallway, as students are excused to use the bathroom. I see her walk in the front door of the building. She steps into the main hall, looks left and right. She has the same high cheekbones, the same coal-black hair that my mother had as a child (my mother gave up that black hair for a dyed, platinum blonde). My grandmother even has the same wiry walk.

She *wires* over. There's a frustration in her walk. She is standing directly in front of me looking bothered: "Little boy," she says, "do you know where the principal's office is?"

Little boy, I think, like an indictment.

I say to her: "Grandma, it's me."

"Oh," she says.

She grabs me by the hand, takes me to her car, and drives me to her trailer in the neighborhood called Heavener Acres. We do not discuss the fact that she did not know who I was. I wonder as I lay on her couch what she knows about me. Does she even know my middle name? My age?

When my mother picks me up later, there is no great catching up between the two of them. I can't even recall a hug.

My mother puts me in the car and drives me toward home. I tell her about the incident in the middle-school hallway. She shakes her head and says she is not surprised.

When we get home, my mother puts me on the couch, kisses my forehead, and wraps me in a blanket. She squeezes my hand much harder than usual. She says my grandmother does not matter. My mother says that she loves me—she looks me in the eye and grabs me by the shoulders—she says that's what matters. She says she doesn't understand this woman. She says she will probably never understand her. She says her mother never cared about her. She kisses and pets me. "But I love you," she says to me. She lingers at my side. It seems like she will never let me go.

To understand my mother is to understand her relationship with my father. It's to understand why they remained married for fifty years, despite the fact that within a week of marriage, she found him in the back seat of a car with a young woman from the local college. She has always told this story proudly. I can picture her eyebrows moving up and down as she tells me the point: "I got that hussy kicked out!"

The young coed begat a series of what must have been at least a dozen affairs, some of which stretched on for years at a time. Their names are beginning to slip from my mind, but I can still hold onto the major ones that crossed some section of my childhood. There was Brenda. There was Mary. And there was, of course, Janet. Janet was a relation of my mother—a distant cousin of some sort. She was Janet with the red hair—fiery locks that I'd seen my mother yank in the middle of the street, in the checkout lane of the grocery store.

Our town was small. My mother's few friends knew what was happening with my father, and these same friends were always offering advice. Leave him. Set yourself free. Begin anew. She alternated between a few states of existence: defensive embarrassment; a vicious, injured wife; a soul-beaten devotee to God.

My mother took no one's advice. Instead, she prayed.

She was just out of high school when she got a job behind the counter at Neale's Drug Store, right at the busiest corner of downtown Elkins. She had an apartment upstairs, where she watched the people come and go in what had then been a bustling little metropolis with multiple department stores, a movie theater, and a working railyard. Mr. Neale himself saw her potential. He told her that she had talent, an eye for beauty. He wanted to send my mother to cosmetology school.

My mother said that, back then, no man had ever treated her right. She said that one day my father walked in, and he saw her there behind the counter. He said he couldn't bear the thought of any man having her. She had been flattered by his passion.

It wasn't long before they were wed. It was a tiny affair. They eloped across the border in Maryland because, in her words, "at that time Maryland didn't require a blood test," which is to say that it was cheap, that it was easy. The Maryland Marriage Index shows them as having been married on November 27, 1965, just a little more than two weeks after her nineteenth birthday. He was twenty-two.

They came home and, presumably, my father met the college woman at some bar or some party. In the early weeks of December 1965, my mother saw them in the back seat of a car. I can't remember if it was his car or the car of the young woman. I don't know how my mother knew to look for them, but my father was always brazen.

My mother would raise a fist or a finger when she told the story. It was *that hussy* or *that little bitch.* My mother viewed her intervention as a victory, the woman's dismissal from the college as justice. The woman had been put in her place. The woman should have known better.

My mother packed my father's lunch nearly every day of his working life. She washed his clothes. She raised his children. She chased his women. She made his breakfast. They were married for fifty years.

"He never really loved me," she told me once, sitting across from me on a picnic table in the Elkins City Park. This was a year or two after my father's death; he died in 2016. She was recounting how they met in Neale's Drug Store, remembering again how Mr. Neale was going to make her a cosmetologist, how my father couldn't stand the thought of someone else having my mother. "He didn't love me, even then. He wanted to possess me."

As a child my father took me to the Moose Club, the local branch of the fraternal order where he managed the bar in his spare time. He would sit me on the bar itself, or he'd let me run around the big event hall, where some other parents also let their kids roam. Typically, he'd never spend more than fifteen or thirty minutes in the front room, where the bar itself was. He'd chat for just a little bit. He'd check with the bartender about the cash situation, about the liquor and booze. Nancy, the bartender, sounded like she'd smoked cigarettes since she'd been born. She'd squeeze my cheeks, give me a Coke, and say, "Jonathan, you're so sweet," and "Jonathan, you're so shy." When all was in order, when I'd been given chips and a drink, he'd dart to the back room, where they kept the pool table and the gambling machines.

My dad loved to gamble, but he did not like physical cards. He only played video poker—particularly five-card draw. I can still hear the rapid click, click, click, click, click—a sound for each card that was dealt. When I was a kid, before the state legislature legalized and regulated these gambling boxes in 2001, they were called "Gray Machines," and they proliferated semilegally in places like the back room of the Moose Club.

My father didn't know what to do with me. I didn't like baseball, and I had failed at hunting—I refused to pull the trigger; I couldn't kill the deer—so he brought me with him to the Moose Club, and I ran around until I got tired. When I was done with the running, I would sit on a tall barstool beside him and watch him gamble away an entire week's paycheck. Sometimes he'd guide my fingers to the screen and tell me which cards to keep, which to discard. It wasn't just any pair, but jacks or better to earn back your bet.

He'd been a wrestler, a football player, a ladies' man. What we had together, if we had anything at all, were Sunday drives in his truck and life lessons at the poker machine. Sometimes he'd let me choose the cards, and I think he began to see then that there was something turning in my mind, some kind of logic forming that he might be able to respect, even if I didn't talk much, even if I couldn't throw a baseball.

"You have to risk something to earn something," he'd say, as we drew for the straight or the flush. What was the point of just getting your money back, after all? Why even play?

He'd explain the difference between the possible hands, the payouts. We wanted the holy grail—the royal flush. He said, "She'll always be miserable." And then he'd say it again in a hundred different ways. I don't think he was trying to defend his actions.

We should have had a working-class life. We never would have been rich, but we shouldn't have been so poor, always just a paycheck away from losing our house. He was a construction worker, and he never missed a day of work. And yet we were always so close—just one bad run with the poker machine and we might not have a roof over our heads or food on the table.

He'd lose $500 on a single Sunday afternoon. He'd say, "Don't tell your mother."

On a good day, he'd win a hundred. He'd pocket forty for himself and put the rest in the white envelope where he kept the hundred-dollar bills after cashing his check. With a wink, he'd say, "Our little secret."

My mother worked odd jobs most of her life, and by the time I was an adolescent, she was the janitor at the local newspaper and she cleaned private homes. For her labor, she was paid at or slightly above minimum wage.

She'd hold out what was left in the white envelope and say, "Jack, I can't make this work."

And he'd say, "What are you spending the money on?"

The credit card debt crept up. It went from $10,000 to $20,000 to $30,000. We had caller ID, and all of us kids understood that when it read "unavailable," we were to hang up the phone quickly so that my father wouldn't find out about the bill collectors.

He blamed her for everything. He'd say, "Woman, why can't you keep it together," and "Woman, why do you have a spending problem," and "Woman, you just really can't let anything go," and then he'd storm out of the house, start the engine to his pickup truck, and drive back to the bar, to one of his not-so-secret girlfriends.

She would cry. She'd throw her hands up. And yet, somehow, credit card bills or not, I never missed a meal. I had a roof over my head.

My father was the kind of man who wanted to have everything—the friends, the girlfriends, a wife who prepared three meals a day—and that's what he got.

She held yard sales to pay for my field trips. She secretly emptied my savings account to buy groceries. One day, when I was a teenager and my sisters had long ago moved out, she told me to get into the car. I asked her where we were going, and she said wait and see.

We drove through the neighborhood by the college, now a historic district, and we pulled up to a two-story house that I'd driven by dozens of times before. It was not large, but it was old and beautiful and seemed like a mansion to me. The real estate agent was waiting for us, and he guided us inside.

It was $70,000. This would have been in 2002 or 2003. I remember at the time how large that number seemed to me. My parents' combined income was less than $35,000.

There were three bedrooms. There were hundred-year-old wooden floors. There was no furniture. The house was vacant. It was a blank slate.

She said, "There's room for you and me."

I said, "Please, please, please, let's do it."

When I was young, I thought anyone who lived in a house with a staircase, with a second floor, was rich.

She said, "I don't know. I don't know how we could make it happen."

I said, "Divorce him. Sell the house. I'll work. Get alimony."

She said, "I just don't know."

We only stayed at the house for fifteen minutes. The realtor left us alone to explore. In that fifteen minutes, I had built a whole new life.

As we drove home, I begged and begged and begged. I could see in her eyes that she'd allowed herself to picture it—just like me—that whole new life. But before we pulled into our driveway, her eyes lost their shimmer. She said, "Don't tell your father."

It was around the same time as the house tour that she saw a sign on a billboard for the state's gambling addiction hotline. The state legalized gambling parlors in 2001, and soon there were more than a dozen such places in my town. They were little holes in the wall with ten or twelve machines, with clandestine parking around the back of the building. My mother must have driven by those places, tortured as each new joint hung a sign, taunted by the billboard's plea to seek help. The sign was up, and there were commercials on the television. There was a stern voice that said something like, "If you or a loved one suffer from a gambling problem, please call . . ."

She told me she had finally broken down. She'd called the 800 number.

She'd told the counselor how much money she made, how much money we owed, and how much my father spent. They'd asked her if she had any outside support, any friends who could help. She'd told them no.

Hers was a tough situation, the counselor had said. The counselor told her to put away a little money each week. The counselor said this was important—that she had to keep the money hidden. The counselor said when she'd saved up enough money—it might be months, it might be years down the road—my mother should run. She should take the money, get in the car, and never turn back.

I begged her to listen. I begged her to make a plan.

She could never see more than a few days ahead.

I left for college. Before long, I learned that my mother had thrown in the towel. There was no money hidden in her sock. My sister Jackie called me, irate. She told me our mother had developed a new problem, that she too had started gambling. And I could see the two of them—him and her—driving around the town, parking in the back lots, sneaking into the little gambling parlors, hiding from each other, spending the little money they didn't have, hoping they'd hit the jackpot that would save their lives.

She'd already disowned me when I discovered what I thought was an error on my credit card bill. I was a sophomore in college, and I always paid my bill online. I was shocked to see the large figure. I owed nearly $2,000 more than I expected. At first I thought someone had stolen my identity.

I called the credit card company. A cash advance check, the representative said, cashed in Elkins, West Virginia. Yes, they confirmed, my permanent address was still listed as Weese Street back in Elkins. Yes, they confirmed, the cash advance checks would have been sent to the Elkins address. Did I want to report fraud?

She was still at that point calling me every odd morning to tell me I was dying of AIDS.

I called her, and it rang and rang and rang and then went to voicemail—my own voice still on the machine: "You've reached the Corcorans . . ."

I called back over and over and over until she finally picked up.

I didn't give her a chance to speak. I was furious.

I said, "Did you cash a check on my credit card? Did you fake my signature?"

She began to sob. She said, "What do you want me to do? What was I supposed to do?"

"Mother!" I shouted. I was fuming.

"What do you want me to do?" she said, her voice breaking. "Do you want me to eat?"

Do you want me to eat. It was such a simple statement, but the words crushed me. I was so confused, trying to think about money, about boundaries, about fairness.

I softened my tone. I said, "If you need money, you should have—"

She cut me off. "Leave me alone," she screamed. "Leave me alone! I'm paying it back."

She hung up the phone.

When I checked the record, I noticed that she had in fact been paying the minimum payment, the twenty-something dollars. And each month going forward, she always mailed in a check. She was never late.

When I got my college loan refund check the next fall—the one that was supposed to pay for my food and housing—I used a large portion to pay off the remainder of the bill. I was living with Sam. I knew, at the very least, that I would always have someone who would make sure that I was fed.

She never again mentioned the money, and neither did I.

7

When I was in college and was left on my own, I'd take her vicious calls in the morning and sometimes I'd cry all day. I'd do my schoolwork the best I could, though my grades were falling and I'd written to my professors for extensions of extensions. I'd write essays on Shakespeare, I'd write essays on European history, and I'd write essays on Toni Morrison, and I'd sit down in my bed when the classes had ended and the assignments had been handed in, finally alone, because maybe Sam was out for an evening, and I'd try to put the literary analysis away for a moment and try to understand how to make her understand.

She kept saying that I was going to go to hell, that I needed to make right with God. I couldn't tell her that I had stopped believing in God, that if God were real, if he had created me and he had created her and he had filled both of our minds with such different thoughts, then God was cruel, unforgiving. I couldn't tell her because I knew, even then, that her anger was only partially about a supposed sin, that there was something deeper—the cycles of abuse, the cruel men in her life—her stepfather, my father—that God was the thing that kept her from driving her car off the cliff. I could not tell her I didn't believe in God, because a part of me feared that if I did so, her only remaining foundation would crack. The foundation was flawed, certainly, but it was what she had, and I was not convinced that there was anything else left to hold the fragility of her health, her mind, her body, her emotions. I had to let her keep God, and I had to find a way to use God in my favor.

This was the curse, has always been the curse for a child—to begin to see the world with a clarity that your parents lack, to begin to see the underpinnings of their actions and choices. I was cast aside, pushed to the brink emotionally, monetarily, physically. While I should have been focused on my healing, on forging a new life without blood parents, I instead began to dwell on her, on her reasons, on how to convince her, as if this was an argument or, even bigger than that, a war. I needed her to see what I saw, and I began to think that I could take the twenty years of her mother's love and squeeze what was left of this love into logic.

What she needed to see was that I was part of God's plan for her, and not just a test, but a thing that fit, that belonged with her vision of how divinity worked, that I too was part of the reward for the suffering she had undergone while trying to survive, while trying to keep a family together, fed, and functioning. I found myself, an atheist—I could say that word to my friends now, even if I would not say it to her—plunged into the logic and illogic of spirituality. This became a quiet but all-consuming obsession.

I would dig into the Bible and find the verses that would speak to her if I could just keep her on the phone a few minutes longer. First Corinthians 13:13: "And now these three remain: faith, hope and love. But the greatest of these is love." And the greatest commandment, Mark 12:30–31: "'Love the Lord your God with all your heart and with all your soul and with all your mind and with all your strength.' The second is this: 'Love your neighbor as yourself.' There is no commandment greater than these." The problem was that the kinds of arguments that would have convinced a religious version of me were not the kinds of things that would work on her—this hatred, these fears were so deeply attached to her core, to the belief system that kept her waking up in the morning. Her convictions were based in the kind of evangelical faith that required she resist questioning, even if said questioning was based on the texts of the religion itself.

There were online discussions and treatises and videos about the true meaning of Sodom and Gomorrah, of the true crime that caused God to destroy the cities. Scholars said the misunderstanding had been one of hospitality, and that, likewise, the verses in Leviticus had to do with cleanliness, not with gay sex per se. I read through all of these—read entire books, shipped copies of these books to my mother—even though I feared that this line of arguing would fall on deaf ears or, worse, would inflame her, that making such points would further her distrust of scholars (she sometimes blamed my gayness on Brown University). I worried that such arguments would make her even more convinced that certain groups of people were hell-bent on manipulating the word of God. There were verses for this mistrust, too, and I could see her fingering the acid-bent pages of Revelation 22:18–19: "I warn everyone who hears the words of the prophecy of this scroll: If anyone adds anything to them, God will add to that person the plagues described in this scroll. And if anyone takes words away from this scroll of prophecy, God will take away from that person any share in the tree of life and in the Holy City, which are described in this scroll." All she had left in the world were dreams of this "Holy City."

I sent her the books and I sent her cards and letters with the gentle verses—the ones about love and about faith and about leaving the judgment to God. But I began to read the Bible more for myself than for her. It wasn't that I needed God—I didn't; I don't—it was that I needed to find some meaning in what was happening, to find some way of seeing all this from a better angle. I was burnt out, and so tired from sifting through the fire and brimstone.

What I found was a coincidence. Even if I didn't believe in God, I could wrap my head around a beautiful happenstance. The happenstance was my namesake, which came from the Bible itself. Jonathan David. I was named, perhaps, without too much thought—she never said that she was drawn to the characters themselves, just the sounds, the idea that Jonathan meant "God's greatest gift"—and that's what I had once been to her. But there it was. There I was. Jonathan and David, perhaps one of the Bible's few examples of same-sex lovers. Yes, lovers. It's sacrosanct for some to consider, but I read through First and Second Samuel like some kind of tragic play. I wept, felt my skin crawl with the eroticism, would close my eyes and inhabit their bodies. I didn't care if some argued that they were only friends, said that the Bible spoke only of a deep friendship. I saw in their story only love and lust.

I would flip through the translations, finding the nuance that felt most relevant—there was a *covenant* made, there was a knitting of souls. They were *bound* together, the bond sealed with ceremonial stripping of Jonathan's robe, his belt, his sword—the garments and weapon handed to David—one man naked in front of the other. What was important was that "Jonathan made a covenant with David because he loved him as himself." It was so pure and honest—how, when Jonathan would die in battle, David would lament: "Your love to me was wonderful, surpassing the love of women."

I would read these verses and reread these verses—of kings, of warriors, of two of the most well-regarded men in the Bible—and I would find in their story, in my own story, a nobility, and I would think to myself, I was always gay, I was meant to be gay, I was born to inherit this story. And though it's a somewhat discomforting thing to admit, there was an autoerotic power that surged through my body as I read this story—naked, in my own bed, in front of the mirror, I was not just a victim, not just the cast-out child. They were men—I was them, I was a man. I would touch the hair on my chest, and touch the curve at my hip, and I would imagine handing my robe to David, who was also me, and handing my sword to him—and, naked and alone, reading the Bible, finding power in the thing that was supposed to harm me, I began to assert myself, the part of myself that had been hidden for twenty years. I was a fully formed man, a body, a soul, a being with sexuality, capable of love and lust.

What my mother and all the bigots hated the most was that our sexuality was real, was visible—the thought of penetrative sex, of phalluses, of body hair, of musks, of sinew.

When I thought of them—these two men, my namesakes, whom I could only see as lovers—the shame receded. I, my bodily self, contained everything that I ever needed. It was foretold. I was not just a survivor. The words had always been there. This was my legacy. In them, I saw that I could be alive, living.

There was always the problem of the sexuality itself, of the sex. After some months of the vile morning phone calls, she would feel guilty and lonely. She would try to get me to adhere to an impossible set of rules.

"I don't need to hear about it," she'd say.

What she meant was relationships, was dating, and was, of course, the sex. She said all this despite both of my sisters consistently being extraordinarily open with her about their own sex lives. I could remember my sister Teresa, always a free spirit, counting off the number of lovers to my mother. She'd slept with more than a hundred men, and my mother would laugh at this—"Oh, Teresa!" But I was not my sister. My mother said that I could come back for Christmas—at a certain point, she begged. We could just not talk about it, she said.

"You could be that person up there, and here, you could be the other person."

She was always splitting me—the child she thought she had known and the version that had been tainted. She always had a suspect in mind—the community theatre, Brown University, New England, even herself—always had some entity or some person who had fouled the child who had once thought of becoming a preacher.

But even though I was hurting—even though I was, in many senses, fractured and fragile—I was beginning to become empowered. The dam had broken. I'd said the word aloud. I was gay. I was the legacy of namesakes—Jonathan and David. I was becoming, I believed, a free soul, had started to live without the weight of guilt and subterfuge.

"I can't exist like that," I told her. "You have to accept that I'm gay, that I have relationships with men."

"Why can't you just . . ." and there was always something. *Be content. Respect my rules. Keep your secrets secret.*

But I had drawn a line in the sand. She herself had chosen to open the floodgates with that awful phone call on my twentieth birthday. "It's all or nothing," I told her. "I hope that one day you'll take me just as I am."

Just as I am. I wondered, when I said that, if she thought then of her favorite hymn.

There had been too many near misses, too much pain from living in the dark, and I didn't want to hurt that way ever again. I'd had what could barely be considered relationships with a number of men when I'd lived back home in West Virginia, when I'd been a teenager. Some of these meetings were benign—clandestine sexual encounters with boys from high school, with the cute guy I'd met from All State Choir. I'd drive my car to whatever secret place was easiest. An older classmate's grandma was out of town once, so we frolicked on the grandma's couch. Later, I'd find myself in a McDonald's parking lot two hours down the Interstate. I'd meet the choir boy in another parking lot, this one opposite a town's underused city park.

And there were darker, formative moments. Like the older man who'd seen me pumping gas, who had followed me down the main road through town. I could see his hungry eyes in the rearview mirror. I'd nervously pulled over, into the McDonald's parking lot (how many McDonald's parking lots could there possibly be in my early life?). I'd rolled down my window, and he said hello. He was attractive, at least thirty. I was sixteen. He handed me a small piece of paper with what I presumed to be his phone number, he nodded, and then he drove away. I'd call him that week, and we'd chat for a while until we got to what it was that he wanted—which was for me to come over—and when I'd get there, we'd hook up in a way. We rolled around naked on his living room floor—literally rolled, touching and wrestling, writhing on his carpet. I didn't know anything, how to do it better. I had no examples, despite my mother's theories of all the things that had tainted me. We rolled and writhed and neither of us finished because I felt too guilty, too sick at my stomach to roll around further. I put on my clothes, drove home, and never spoke to him again.

Later that same year, I'd go to American Legion Boys' State, and I'd become shocked to see that the naked man was the director of the camp facility where we stayed, how he was in charge of a camp with hundreds of teenage boys, how he turned in shame when I, a minor, caught his eyes.

Of course I had never told her anything about that, and of course I lived with those details for years and years—trying to figure out if hooking up with a thirty-year-old man was abusive, was empowering, was important, was shameful. I lived with that and the other close calls, like the man I'd met online, on a chat site in the years before Grindr. I wanted more than anything to experiment with my sexuality, because that's what young people do. I was sixteen or seventeen—definitely not yet an adult—and the man had messaged me on Gay.com and said I was handsome, had proposed we take a drive. The implication was clear, though not stated outright. He was from a few towns over, and we'd meet in a convenient parking lot, this time at a gas station.

I parked my car. He waved from one spot over. I got into his car after the briefest of hellos, and I immediately realized that I was making a bad decision. He looked ten years older than he claimed in his profile. His presence, his muskrat facial hair, made my skin prickle. The sun had set and the sky was dark. But how do you put the brakes on such a thing when no one has ever told you how to navigate your sexuality?

I thought he might murder me. We drove down backroads, headlights rolling up and down the pavement. He put his hand on my thigh. I was repulsed by him physically—there was just something wrong, too eager—and yet his desire, that someone would desire me, turned me on enough to keep letting him run his hands all over me. We drove and he tugged at me like a gearshift. We ended up at a motel, the classic kind with a boxy, column-fronted office and a row of rooms extending down either side. He went to the front desk alone. There was no discussion. I followed him inside the room.

It's easy to feel flattered for no good reason. I had so little money, and here was this man, attracted to me, willing to put what felt like an overly large sum down on a motel room for one evening with me. I was poor, gay, and inexperienced. In that moment I felt turned on, physically attractive, that I was worth something to someone.

My time with the school-aged boys had been on the innocent side of the spectrum. We kissed. We touched. We pushed a little further. Even with the man who rolled with me naked on the floor, we'd stopped before going too far. But this man—a man for whom I felt no real attraction, who seemed older than in his picture—disrobed and directed me to the bed. I don't know why I obliged, but I thought I might as well go through with it, if for no other reason than to strip me of that title that haunts all teenagers. There was very little foreplay. He put me into position—on my knees, on the bed—and tried to ram himself inside me.

I had never had penetrative sex with anyone. He shoved his dick at my ass. In a few seconds, with a little effort, he made it all of an inch—maybe less—and I screamed in pain. I pushed him away, and I moved from the bed and told him that we had to stop, that I wanted to go home.

His face froze, turned a violent red. I thought he might harm me. He went to the bathroom, slammed the door shut. I was naked on the bed, hugging myself. I caught myself in a cheap mirror mounted to the wall. In the yellow light of the motel, I saw exactly how young I appeared.

We dressed. I apologized. He drove me the hour back to my car without saying a single word. I suppose I'm lucky that he took me back, that he didn't drive away alone, that he didn't kick me onto the floor. And yet, during the drive, I remember how I kept saying, "I'm sorry; I'm so, so sorry." What I felt in the moment was that I had failed to follow through, that I had wasted this man's money, and that I was soiled.

He dropped me off at my car, back in the gas station parking lot. I drove the forty minutes home. I had concocted some excuse, that I had been hanging out with some friends, and still, my mother gave me a look—one so on the edge of knowing—that made me want to die. I said good-night to her, and closed my door. I wept into my pillow, unsure if I was still a virgin.

Years later, my mother and I sat at a picnic table in the Elkins City Park. She'd finally heard a few details from my youth that she says she didn't know—mostly stories of bullying, of students and teachers giving me a hard time. She said, "I wish you would have told me. I didn't know how much you hurt."

As time passes, as she nears the end of her life, our relationship will mend just a little. She'll continue to tell herself stories like this, that she would have been there for me if only I would have told her what I needed. She'll die without ever knowing that I was once alone in a dirty motel room with a man whose name I cannot remember, and that I came home to my bedroom and cried myself to sleep while she nursed her suspicions over a cigarette in the darkness.

8

There's a family photo album sitting on my bookshelf in our apartment in Brooklyn. My sister Jackie put it together as a gift to my mother. She'd rummaged through boxes scattered in our closets back home, the boxes forgotten in the big shed back by the creek. She selected bits and pieces from all our lives. There are photos of all of us as babies, as teenagers, at weddings, as growing balls in our mother's womb. There are aunts and uncles and people I don't recognize who have probably long since passed away. There's a rough chronology—from black and white to color, from birth to beyond—though it's not a rigid one.

Sometimes when I'm sitting home by myself or I'm missing them, or sometimes when I'm stewing over the fact that she's gone, attempting to make sense of what happened to us, I'll pull the album out and try to summon memories from times when things seemed, perhaps, less complicated.

It's a green photo album with a stock image of a hazy, yellow rose, and underneath the image, a simple cursive "Photographs." The cover remains wrapped in the original protective film. A sticker adhered to the plastic says: "Pocket Photo Album. Memo area. PVC free, acid free—safe for photos. Holds 3 photos per page." It has roughly the dimensions of a magazine in width and length, but it's much thicker, of course. The album and the memories inside remain frozen in time, wrapped safely in the plastic film that covers each page.

They're physical pictures, and what I mean by that is that they're not digital prints. They were captured on film. Four-by-sixes developed at the drugstore or twenty-four-hour photo place.

Polaroids, faded or fading to sepia. Older photos—squares from cameras and types of film that I couldn't name. There are school photos and season's greetings on postcards. It's so easy to look at those pictures—we're all always smiling—and to draw conclusions, to assume that we were happy.

It's not that we weren't. Why do I say this over and over again? The more I write, the more I grapple. I have this notion that some types of feeling override the others. Sadness, depression, worry, anger. They're like the trump cards of memory. I wrestle and push them away to see the cracks of light that I know also existed. Look at the way my mother holds that baby. Look at the way my sister marches in that wedding dress. My father, in his boxer shorts, sleeps peacefully on the old brown couch. Those moments, those bright, bright moments, existed. Why do I forget them?

I look at the photos. I look at the smiles. There's my mother, dressed as a mouse on Halloween, sitting with her old friend Carolyn and another man I don't recognize at the bar—posing cheekily for the camera. There's something different about the immediacy of the images captured back then. I run my hands over the clingy plastic that covers the pages. I dig my fingers behind the photos and find hidden ones that have slipped behind with time. They're fragile, mostly one of a kind. These photos, arranged in that semblance of order, say we lived.

A student said to me that her mother divorced her father, that the mother purged everything from their joined lives, even the images on her smartphone. But her mother could not get rid of their photo albums—the ones with the physical prints. They had been divorced for more than a decade, if I remember the story correctly, and the student said her mother still held a tiny photo of her and her ex together in her wallet.

The physicality of the album is what throws me. It spurs a memory that I am not sure I believe. A fact: I stole this photo album from my home back in West Virginia. It used to sit inside a bookcase in our old front room, the bookcase in the dim corner across from the only bathroom in the house. Another fact: There was a day when my mother said to me, "I know you took the photo album. You should keep it. I want you to have it." When she said this I do not know, and if the words were uttered in person or over the phone, I could not say. That distinction has become impossible for me. When I remember her words, I see her lips move. When I hear her speak, I am looking into her eyes.

This is the story that I can remember. It is also the one I cannot trust.

I try to place myself. I've been disowned. I've been cut off. I'm alone in Providence, and I'm alone in the world. All the things that have been my birthright—my family, my home, my memories—are gone.

I'm sitting alone in a dorm room or maybe by this time an apartment. I'm in a city so far from my birth. I'm trying to understand, to accept, that this is all I have—the used couch from the street, the books on the shelf, the letters in my desk (but not the old antique desk, the one I love so much and the one she said she'd save for me once I had a big enough space). The memories in my head—they are there, too, but even at this young age, twenty-one or twenty-two, I can sense the pictures of my youth getting fuzzy.

Sometimes, I sit alone on the used couch (green, Victorian, golden, stained) and close my eyes and run down the list. I hear her laugh, hear the crinkle of her dyed-blonde hair. I rub her cracked feet, feel her hand on my back. I smell her nicotine fingers. There is her cup of Lipton tea in the little ceramic mug that is white with flowers around the brim. I taste the milky black tea. And I say, I don't want to lose this all. I don't want to lose what made me. I can feel those things—the images, the senses—going away.

Where was I?

I've left Providence in a rental car. It's the summer, and I'm driving. I'm back in West Virginia. I've gone over the green, green mountains and arrived in town. I've snuck back home to see my friends. I had to see them. It was like a game—trying not to be discovered in a town of 7,000 people, of 3.4 square miles.

I am staying with a friend—Emily, Mandy?—and I wait until the middle of the day. It's a weekday. I've timed this so that my father is at work. I pray that she's gone too.

I've driven through all the streets of the town, looped one end to the other—from the movie theater to Walmart—but I haven't gone back to the house since it happened.

It's not far—just a ten-minute walk from the little brick and block downtown. I'm in my rental car, and I turn off of Randolph Avenue, off of Diamond Street, which my dad said was named for a ballfield that no longer exists. I see the sign. Weese Street. There's the creek that follows the whole street, the creek that flows into the Tygart, into the Monongahela, into the Ohio, into the Mississippi, into the Gulf of Mexico. I call it "the creek," and I used to pronounce it like "the crick," like a crick in your neck, until my second-grade teacher told me I would speak "properly" and made me repeat her proper words until I no longer sounded like the other kids from Weese Street. I have learned from looking at Google Maps that "the creek" supposedly has a name—Wees Run, spelled, inexplicably, without the extra E of Weese Street. Wees Run. Weese Street.

My face burns, I feel hot and dizzy, as I turn the corner onto Weese Street, as I catch sight of Wees Run. All I've done for the past year, alone at college, without her, is think about these things. The past looms so large in my mind—it accretes with all the sadness, loss, nostalgia—and yet, turning the corner, everything looks smaller. The houses. The woods that rise up on both sides of the street. There were so many big trees in my memories—the maple trees as tall as California redwoods.

I'm seeing fractals. The woods that rise up on both sides of the road make Weese Street a microcosm of the town itself. A valley within a valley. Everything meanders. The creek. The hillside. The road. The town. The mountains. The highways. My memories.

I am driving slowly at first, keeping a safe visual distance. We are the third house on the left—that's what we used to say, before the Internet, before GPS. I was eleven or twelve and I gave out invitations to a summer party—there was no reason for the party itself—no birthday, no holiday—except we wanted to get wet. We wanted to throw water balloons. We wanted to squirt water guns and jump in the creek. *Turn the corner. It's the third house on the left.* I lean the driver's seat back—just far enough so that my head is blocked by the slice of the car's frame, the bar between the driver's window and the rear-passenger window. I speed up. I pray that she doesn't see me driving by, that the neighbors don't see me and tell her I was there.

I steal a glance, and in the rearview mirror I can confirm it. My father's truck is not there. There is no car in the driveway. No one is home. My plan is working.

I drive up the street until I find a spot to turn the car around. We live on a dead-end street, and I can still remember which neighbors get angry when people use their driveways to turn around. By the time I left high school, I was tired of angry neighbors. I started turning my car around in the middle of the road.

I am approaching the house again. It's a little box of a place—truly. My house and my neighbor's identical house used to be army barracks, little metal boxes placed on the campus of Davis & Elkins College, where soldiers or officers would stay while they trained for World War II. The houses were part of the West Virginia Maneuver Area—some 100,000 soldiers passed through. The men climbed up, flew over, and shot ordnance toward the Allegheny Mountains. The terrain was said to resemble the mountains of Italy. My mother swore she saw ghosts in the hallways, the devil's red eyes out the kitchen window. Ghosts, soldiers, demons.

My chest tightens as I approach, as I'm hit with memories of being cooped up in my room worrying over spirits of all sorts. I pull into the driveway. I step out of the car and I take it in. I look to the roof, the little octagon window, the makeshift attic created when my father built an addition—he placed one roof over the other, so that the angles framing the house seem far too complicated for a house that size. I'm nervous that I'll get caught, so I only allow myself a few seconds to see and remember: the grass in the front yard, the lightning bugs, the front porch with the tin roof, thunderstorms in the evening.

Am I holding my breath?

The door is unlocked. She has never in my entire life locked the front door.

Inside it's an assault. The smells of stale cigarette smoke and potpourri. The pilot light of the gas heater on the wall. The dining room table with the white tile surface. The low ceiling, only a few inches taller than Sam, my "good friend." *Watch the ceiling fan,* she'd told him.

It's all as I remember. The creaking wooden floors. The wall of mirrors. The country-kitsch decor. The furniture has been moved just a little. The couch pushed over there by the wall.

This is my home. This was my home. My heart is beating quickly. There is so little time.

I walk into the kitchen, and I see her ashtray and her ashes and the butts. I see a coffee cup in the sink. There's the faint smell of my father's coffee pot. There's the dim little window that looks out onto the creek, the woods.

I run my hand over every surface. There's no time. I have to feel everything.

I head back into the front room, cross to the place I'm afraid to look.

My door is open. My bed is there. My trophies are on the desk. My pictures are on the wall. My books are on the shelf. My old clothes are in the closet. I am there. I am frozen in time.

I feel as if I could pass out. I feel as if I will be arrested. There is no time.

What I want more than anything is to remember this. What I want more than anything is not to lose a sense of this place, this place that holds my memories. I can't stand seeing it, and I don't want to stop looking.

I have to leave before someone comes home. I have to leave before she finds me. Something tells me I have only minutes.

I leave the bedroom, and there's the bookshelf in the dim corner with all my old novels. What am I looking for? And I see it—the photo album. I remember the photo album. We were so bad at doing things like this, at organizing our lives, our histories. My sister tried. She tried to make sense of it. Jackie took the piles of our memories and arranged them.

I don't know what I'm doing. I grab the photo album. I run out the front door. I get into my rental car. I drive away.

I am crying. I am alone again. I am haunted by what I have seen.

But I have the photo album. Now, I will remember.

I do not trust my memory.

Let me demonstrate.

On the first page of the photo album, my sister Teresa appears to be maybe eight or nine and she sits with another girl on a donkey at the edge of the street in front of our house. An older man steadies them. I do not recognize the young girl or the man. On the back of the photo I see their names—Henry, Teresa, Annette. That's all it takes. Henry and Annettte, our neighbors just a few houses down. The faces now appear in my memory, as if I were there, as if I were yet born.

Why is she sitting on a donkey? This is a question I've asked before, and I know that my mother or my father once gave me an answer. I want to say that they told me that the neighborhood was different then, that the man who lived next door or maybe two houses down had once kept a small collection of farm animals. We lived within city limits, and I have never known anyone to keep such animals in the town—in fact, I recall there being a regulation against it.

Was it even a donkey? A mule? A small pony?

I search the Internet for images of mules and tiny ponies and donkeys, and still I am unsure. My inability to determine even this small fact vexes me, and the more I look at the photo, the more I become resigned to not knowing.

There is an easy enough solution. I can call up my sister and ask her. She will no doubt tell me what she can remember from that time. And what will she remember, Teresa, who is soon turning fifty, about the reason a neighbor was allowed to keep a farm animal within city limits?

What I know is that when I tell people about the story of the photo album, I tell them about how lonely and sad I was, and how my blood was pumping when I went into that house, and how I was so surprised to find my room intact—that maybe subconsciously I took this little detail that my things had not been thrown out as a sign that there was still hope that my mother and I might make amends.

And this fits so nicely into the narrative of being a child abandoned, of this all being some grand adventure of survival. It's so dramatic, almost heroic, trying to imagine myself driving down that street, running into that house, risking so much.

Here is the problem: Why now, as I flip through this photo album, do I see a photograph of Sam in a graduation cap and gown dated May 2014, which is the year that he graduated with a doctorate in psychology from Rutgers? Why is there a photograph tucked into this album from the year 2014, which is roughly a decade after I recall stealing the album from my old home?

I am not the kind of person to slip photographs into an old photo album. I have asked Sam. He did not add this photograph into the album. He is adamant about this fact.

I remember driving down that street. I remember sneaking into that house. I remember years later my mother saying that she knew I stole the photo album, telling me to keep it.

What am I missing? How did the photo get there?

I begin to distrust my own memory. I begin to ask myself, if I can't trust my own recollection of events, how am I ever supposed to make sense of what happened to us? And further—was I wrong about everything?

I could drive myself mad thinking like this. I try to quiet the cacophony of contradiction.

I am only human. Memory is a lived thing. Memory is a felt thing. What I felt was real.

I look at the photographs. I recite the stories behind the images I see, like a litany in church, to keep the spirit of my memory alive.

PART TWO

9

I tell Sam that this is harder than I expected. It's the beginning of summer, a year and change after her death, and for the first time since she passed, I'm not teaching. Each morning I wake up at eight or nine and try to get to this as fast as possible. I avoid the news. I try to avoid my email. I get straight to the shower and the coffee and then her.

"I sit here all day and think about her," I say to Sam, the therapist. "It's all a little depressing," I say clinically, like I'm discussing a dramatic television show or the latest statistics about climate change. He is sympathetic in spite of, or maybe because of, his job. He closes the door and takes his work all in, never revealing the details—ethics, of course. Maybe he'll say *That last one was having a really hard time* or *This case is really challenging* or *I am glad I have you*. He has become a master of turning it on and off.

Every weekday it's the same. Wake up, shower, coffee, reminisce, relive. I close my eyes for an hour, walk through the hot sun, come back to the desk, recover.

It's claustrophobic work. I crave new vistas. I begin to spend my mornings in Mount Prospect Park—a little pocket park with a circular walking path. Mount Prospect is adjacent to the much bigger, much more trafficked Prospect Park. I prefer the smallness of Mount Prospect, how I see the same nannies and the same old women and the same stressed-out dads smoking joints up on the shaded benches by the back fence. There's a comfort in their presence, in how they make the big city feel so much more familiar.

I've become fond of the little yellow notepad that comes standard with iPhones. Like the little park itself, there's a comfort in the smallness of the screen. I sit on a bench, and I pull up the yellow notepad, and some days I type whole memories, whole chapters. Some days I get stuck on a single phrase. Today is Wednesday, June 16. It's one week before I will pick up a rental car and drive to see my sisters for the first time in a year and a half, a week before I will see the tree where my mother's ashes have been sprinkled. Today I write: "You'll never let me forget anything I've done."

She used to say this frequently, but I am remembering a particular moment. I have already graduated college. I can't remember the exact year, but I'm likely in my late twenties. We are attempting to repair our relationship again, to find some middle ground. We are sitting in the Elkins City Park at a picnic table underneath the big oak trees that seem to drop thousands of acorns all year long. We have sat like this in the park before and we will sit there again, year after year, the same mission. I think of these times as our moments of détente, where we agreed to set aside our differences in hopes of fixing things once and for all.

"You'll never let me forget anything I've done."

And I guess what she says is true, because when she says this, I refuse to meet her at our house because I am still scared of her, in a way.

I keep running through the moments of our past like a scratched record that keeps repeating the same phrase: "Do you remember."

I say, "Do you remember what you said to me after that fourth-grade Halloween party?"

She says, "I'm sorry."

I say, "Do you remember throwing me back onto the street to fight with Adam?"

She says, "I'm sorry. What do you want me to say?"

I say, "Do you remember what you said to me in the apartment with Mandy?"

And there isn't much more that she can add, so we just stare at each other, and then we gaze off to the kids playing basketball and to the old-timers sitting on the swinging bench. When I was young, we used to sit together on that same swinging bench, arms touching arms, legs touching legs. Now I need the wide distance of a picnic table.

I ask her why, why she did the things she did.

And she says it: "You'll never let me forget anything I've done."

Across one street, we see the good Christians walk in and out of the First Baptist Church. Across another, the college students walk up and down the hill. I do not deny that I won't let her forget anything that she's done. At this point in our relationship, probably our third or fourth estrangement, it is, in fact, those very things that she has done, those very things that I fear she will continue doing, that are the point.

She sighs and says, "I don't know. It's just what I was taught."

I do and don't believe her. I know that my version of masculinity, my understanding of love, is not, as she says, what she was taught. But I also know, can still remember, how deeply she cared for me, how deeply she hurt for me, how forcefully she protected me. And so I cannot believe her when she says it so simply, when she neglects to connect all the dots, when she attributes what happened to a simple matter of upbringing, of education—moral or otherwise.

I do not tell her, but I have made a secret promise to myself that until she examines her actions, until she understands exactly why she did what she did, I won't, as she says, let her forget anything. I will sit with her on picnic tables in the Elkins City Park and hash through the details and remind her of all the things that have happened that have yet to be resolved.

And though I may sound stubborn, vindictive, there is good reason for this: Every time I let her forget, we end up exactly back where we started. Every time I let her forget, we both end up shattered and shell-shocked and crying alone in the dark.

My father once said, "I always knew you were a little different." Or he might have said, "I always knew you were a little funny." I seem to remember him saying both. The implication was the same.

She would have known. Of course she would have known. I was too feminine as a child. I was interested in the wrong activities.

My father wanted me to play baseball, and I did for a while—surviving tee-ball, aging out of minor league because I wasn't good enough to earn a spot in little league.

I was interested in doing gymnastics, like my neighbor Kristen. She was a few years older, and I viewed her as a goddess. She'd tumble across my yard—round-off, back handspring, back tuck. I'd imitate her and fall on my head and hurt my neck.

My father would grumble. My mother would say, "He's just a kid, Jack." I'd shrug him off, and dance to a VHS my oldest sister owned of Madonna's "Like a Virgin" tour. I'd stand on the couch and lip sync and dip and grab my pretend breasts while my sisters and their friends would hoot and holler. I was not to do this around my father.

I was five or six and I'd throw the ball with him in that same side yard where I preferred to do gymnastics. I'd throw the ball until I'd miss too many times, my arms always seeming to bend at a wide angle. I wasn't trying hard enough, he'd argue. I wasn't putting in any effort. "Damn it, boy," he'd say, and storm off back to the living room to watch television alone.

My mother would see my face, would see the way I retreated into my bedroom, and she'd jump in again to defend me—"He's your son, Jack"—and they would fight while I listened and cried with my head against the bedroom floor.

She'd have known, but she would make excuses. She'd watch me read book after book and say, "He's not a redneck like you, Jack." And maybe this time he would agree. He would come home from work, body aching and tired, skin and hair and t-shirt and jeans covered in concrete and dust. He'd see me sitting there on the couch reading the latest R. L. Stine, and he'd say, "I want you to get an office job."

I had friends on my street. There were at least a half-dozen or so kids around my age. They were fickle and could sometimes be cruel. There was Kristen, who was kind and didn't care if I wanted to talk about Kim Zmeskal or Dominique Dawes, and then there were the boys who liked me when I was useful for their games and grew wary of me when I stepped just a bit too far away from a certain kind of masculinity.

I had been called Jon-Boy for most of my early childhood, but by elementary school this began to morph into Jon-Girl. And I'm sure I told her, and I'm sure that many of those times she would have patted me on the head, told me they were only words, told me yet again not to worry, that God had great plans for me.

He called her "woman." Patty was her name, but you wouldn't know it. It was, "Woman, don't tell me how to raise my kid," and "Woman, don't tell me how to spend Friday night," and "Damn it, woman, you will never, ever be happy. God damn."

Woman, woman, woman. He would say it like that, too, echoing a refrain that was as condescending as it was threatening. No, he never hit her, never laid a finger on her. But he cut away with his words. I am fairly certain that he made her second-guess her own sanity.

What I remember of her is that she would have known, but she didn't say anything. What I remember is that many days she tried to protect me from him and those other boys. And then some days, he would find a way to get to her. He would see me, assess my interests, my choices, my demeanor. He'd wait until I was out of earshot and start. "Woman, woman, woman, what have you done to our son?"

She was my protector and my tormenter. It's hard to find the balance, to understand when she was what and when. I play around with these words, let them roll off my tongue, and try to figure out which one feels more right. She was both, I know.

We would be sitting in the park, another period of détente, trying to hash out our differences. She would work so hard to keep it together—deep breaths, her eyes darting back and forth, from the cigarette in her hand to my tired face. But she couldn't hold back. The anger would build, and then she'd snap. She'd say, "Oh, you just had such a terrible childhood, didn't you."

In some ways, yes, I think. I try to tell her this. I try to tell her that the things she did were damaging. I try to tell her that the things she did to me hurt me and continue to hurt me. I try to relate the details again, retell these horrid stories, in hopes that she might genuinely apologize, that she might not just shoot out deflective vitriol.

I'm remembering Adam. He was a neighbor boy who lived in a trailer up the street. He's my same age, give or take a month. Adam's dad ran in the same circle as my father. They were friends from bars, good ol' boys from the good ol' days. When Adam and I were friends, my father was still relatively young. He had a reputation—he was rough and tumble, a bar fighter. He told a hell of a good joke, was a man who kept his word. There were at least two types of people in our town back then, and my dad was one of those types and Adam's dad was the same.

I'm remembering childhood. I'm remembering Adam. He and I are sometimes friends and sometimes enemies. I can't be more than eight or nine. It's summer. Yesterday we were probably jumping on his trampoline. Today we are currently on enemy status. We've had some kind of fight. I've gone from Jon-Boy to Jon-Girl again. Adam is screaming at me and shoving me. I'm retreating back toward home.

This is the early nineties, and to be gay, to be feminine here, is to be diseased, is to be synonymous with AIDS. I am Jon-Girl, not quite gay, but suspect. I am running down the street trying to avoid getting hit in the face, and I am saying things like, "I won't fight you" and "I don't believe in violence." This is West Virginia, is Elkins, is Weese Street, so the neighbors are watching from their porches and no one is intervening. Adam has a reputation for trouble. Like my father, he has a reputation for using his fists to solve problems. I don't fully understand the extent of it yet, but I am developing a different kind of bad reputation—that suspect part of me, that difference, that thing that marks me.

It's an awkward thing to fight in the street, even more awkward to fight when one party is not interested. Adam shoves me. I am walking backward, and he shoves me, and I steady myself. I face him, and turn to walk and run, and he catches up with me and shoves me again. He lives about a quarter-mile up the street, and we repeat this all the way from his trailer to my front door—shove, walk, run; shove, walk, run. The heat rises from the asphalt, trails me down the street. I am dizzy and anxious.

I finally make it home. I run into my house, and Adam is in the middle of the road yelling obscenities at me and challenging me to fight him. He will not cross the threshold into my house—not with my father and his reputation. My father asks what the hell is going on, and I explain that we are fighting over something stupid and that Adam is not going to stop but I have no interest in fighting him. My father says, *Get back out there and fight him, don't be a pussy, prove yourself.* And I say, "Violence isn't the answer," which is something I've heard and something I understand is a little trite but also strikes me as deeply true. My father grabs me by the shoulders and shoves me out the front door, off the front porch, and when I try to come back inside, he is standing there blocking my way.

She's standing there, right up behind him, right against my father's shoulders, and I look to her, not to him, and say, "I don't want to fight, Mommy, please."

She shakes her head. She says to do what your father says, prove this for your father. She has this vicious look in her eyes, a look that says this is nonnegotiable, that says other things I am too young to comprehend.

The front doorway is blocked by both of their bodies. I beg and plead but they stand there, his big chest, her piercing eyes. Adam is in the street yelling and beckoning. I can hear the neighbors shouting. One shouts, "Kick his ass, Jon." The neighbors, like my mother, want to see me prove that I am not suspect. They want to give me this chance, to right the great tragedy that is Jack Corcoran having *me* as his only son.

I have no other option. I go into the street, and Adam punches me. I take it, and I think about fighting back, but I don't have it in me. It's not that I don't have it in me, it's that this is my character—even then, at eight or nine. I will stand on this principle. I will not fight back, and he hits me again. I cower back to the front door, but my father won't have it. My father shoves me off, pushes me back toward the road. I have no choice.

Adam pummels me over and over. Eyes, stomach, chin. There's blood. My father and my mother and the neighbors jeer and shout like it's a boxing match. But this match is no match at all. I have made up my mind that I will not fight back, that I won't be the kind of person who uses my fists. I decided it then and there, and it becomes a mantra that I keep, like at eighteen when I become a vegetarian. I am stubborn in this, in all my choices.

The neighbors and my parents watch it all unfold, watch me get punched and kicked, pulped. It can't have lasted more than five or ten minutes. Adam has been hitting a punching bag. And so, after I have been sufficiently battered and bruised, when it is clear to all parties that I *really* am not going to fight him, my father finally steps in and says to Adam, not me, "That's enough. You win."

The last thing I remember from that day is both of my parents making these awful sounds of disgust, how they kept saying they were so, so disappointed in me. They leave me on my own to tend to my wounds.

When I was nine years old I had chronic earaches. She would go to the pharmacy and get the special drops, and she'd sit with me on the bed for hours and hours patting me as I cried the pain away. When I was nine years old, I tried to join my elementary school's basketball team, and when I failed the tryouts, when the coach said I didn't have enough talent, my mother said to ignore such people, that they only cared about things like names and money. She said that I was very special, God's greatest gift, and that one day I was going to change the world.

Also, when I was nine years old, I got this idea that it would be really funny to go to school on Halloween dressed as a woman. My elementary school had planned a Halloween parade to take place during recess. *Mrs. Doubtfire* had recently come out at the movies. Past Halloweens I had been a pirate or a devil. I just couldn't get the idea out of my head.

She told me not to do it, but I insisted. I always had a way of convincing her that my ideas had merit. I'd prepare talking points and make my case like a lawyer. She always told me she was so impressed with how my mind worked. She always told me that I was so smart. That Halloween I went to school in a wig and one of my sister's old dresses.

It didn't take long. At first it was snickering and pointing. The teacher kept most of that under control during class in the morning, but by lunch, by the time the parade started at recess, the boys and even some of the girls let loose. They said, "Faggot, faggot, faggot," and as we walked in that endless circle around the playground, it seemed like they'd never stop.

The teacher or an aide escorted me from the field. I ended up wet-faced, sitting in the principal's office. It was understood that I should be sent home for the day.

My mother arrived at the school and dragged me by the hand to the car. I was mortified, I was ashamed—but I was also glad to be rescued by her. I wanted to go home and hide under the covers, and I wanted her to come into my room and pat my back and tell me that she loved me no matter what.

When she'd gotten into the driver's seat, when we'd both closed our doors, I said, "They called me names."

She started the engine, pounded her palm against the steering wheel. She said, "I told you not to do it."

I couldn't speak.

She fumed on the short ride home—eyes sharp and straight ahead. She sped down the highway, past the strip mall toward town. She didn't even light a cigarette. I was so scared.

At the red light by McDonald's she turned to me and pointed a finger. She said, "I told you not to do it." It seemed like the light would never turn. She said, "Are you a faggot, Jon? Maybe you are a faggot."

We were only six or seven blocks from our house, but she kept saying it over and over—"Maybe you want to be a faggot, maybe you like faggots"—all the way to our driveway. Each time she said it, I'd cry louder.

I walked into the dining room. I was still in a dress. She told me to take off my stupid clothes, to go to my room and think about what I'd done.

I closed my bedroom door. I took off the girl clothes, and I put on my boy clothes.

I began to formulate a mantra: Deep voice. Broad shoulders. Girlfriends. Filthy jokes. Church hymns.

She could see something I couldn't yet understand. I vowed never ever to let the cracks show. It was a losing battle.

10

That first Christmas after she had disowned me, she told my father that I'd gone to study abroad in Paris. Before we had become estranged, I had told her that studying French in Paris was my dream, and that I was hoping to find a way to make it work in spite of the fact that neither of us had money to spare on such frivolity. And it was frivolity, I knew. I took French for six years, but there was college tuition to be paid. There was money for food and groceries and clothes that I just didn't have. That summer, the last one we ever spent together, I had come back to West Virginia and gone to the dentist in pain, and the dentist had told me that I had more than $10,000 worth of work to be done. My mother had thrown her hands up, had cried, had suggested I take out credit cards. I researched every clinic, every charity—but I continued to come up with more of the same. My mouth was broken, and there was nothing to be done. Bad teeth, bad debt, bad luck. I knew there would never be money for Paris.

I found out about the Paris story a couple of years later, when we'd begun our first tentative peace. She told me that my father was still in the dark—that he didn't know I was gay—which I thought absurd and impossible since I had been away for so long. She begged me not to tell him. I hated her for that—that she hadn't had the guts to tell him the truth, that she would invent whole imaginary lives in which I got to do the things I couldn't afford—and I hated myself because something in me agreed to go along with her charade. It wasn't lost on me, even then, what was happening. I was beginning to put the pieces together—to understand that God was part of this, but that another man in her life held as much power as any religious deity. And there was something so complex, so strange, about how she needed me to be a certain version of a man, the kind of man who kept his word, who would treat his wife well, who would raise his children with love and involvement. I was supposed to be all these men rolled into one—the husband she'd always wanted, the father she'd never met. My oldest sister was fourteen years my senior, and my mother had never stopped trying for that son—the one she just knew would fix things. She'd spent all my youth watching me with both awe and fear.

I almost thought it romantic that this fictitious version of me had gone abroad, had become fluent in French, had smoked cigarettes in Le Marais with cute boys. In fact, I had spent Christmas that first year only three miles from home. One of my West Virginia friends, Morgan, had told her mother what had happened to me, what my mother had done, and that I intended to spend Christmas alone. Gerry, Morgan's mom, wouldn't stand for it. She was the kind of person who never had fewer than three or four rescued pets. I imagine she thought of me similarly, which is not to say that she thought of me as pitiful. She loved her animals with all her heart. She believed that all creatures deserved a chance to be happy, and when you saw her pack running around her house—the ears flopping, the barking—you understood that certain people had enough love inside them to make up for a thousand broken souls.

Gerry insisted that I come stay with her. I was in a fatalistic mode for much of that year—determined to be self-reliant, self-sufficient—but something about Gerry's request had pierced me. She said, "I can't understand how any mother would do that to her child." It was such a simple thing to say, and though I was wearing a very hard shell, had shrugged off similar comments from my friends at college, there was something about the fact that she was a mother herself, that she was a grown woman living in West Virginia only a few miles from my own home. I couldn't refuse her, and so Christmas that first year was at Gerry's.

When I arrived at Gerry's, I was greeted warmly, treated with extra care. She fed me, she made me a bed on the couch in the den, and she ensured that I had an equal number of presents under her tree. And it wasn't just the number of presents that was equal—she ensured that I, too, received the same value of gifts as her two children. It was 2004, and in addition to a number of smaller presents, we all received new iPods, which were not cheap at the time. I remember her tucking me in on the couch that Christmas night, and I remember going to sleep with my iPod at my side, the headphones still in my ears.

She said later that she had seen me there on the couch, asleep with my headphones, and that she had been so happy to know that I liked my gift.

And it was true, I did. What I didn't tell her was that I was listening to music on my new device, but what I was hearing was that someone cared enough about me to make sure I didn't fall through the cracks. I cried before sleep that night—briefly, quietly, covertly. I wish I remembered what song got me through the night. I listened to it on repeat—that I remember. I was beginning to see that I might be able to forge a new kind of family after the loss of my own.

There was Sam at my side from the beginning, and friends, but Gerry was perhaps the first person who had pierced me. The more I write this story, and the more I tell my friends and family what exactly it is that I'm writing, what this story is about, the more I'm realizing how easy it is to go completely hard in the face of trauma. When I say hardness, I am referring to the exterior, to one's ability to show vulnerability, to the ability to show any emotion at all.

I was chatting with an old friend from college, Leora, and she said that it was her general understanding that I didn't want to talk about any of this, that I preferred not to discuss what was happening. She wasn't wrong, I suppose, but I am realizing now also that what I allowed myself to show and what I was actually feeling were so far apart that I might as well have been living in two bodies—the one internal and the other external. Or maybe it's better to say that there were three—the self I showed to others, the self I thought I knew, and the self that was in preservation mode, not just unwilling to reveal itself, but incapable—the kind of preservation bred from necessity.

11

It's Monday morning, a week before the summer solstice, and I am standing naked in the bathroom preparing to cut my hair. I have mostly gone bald, so cutting my hair means running the Wahl clippers in haphazard rows across my scalp until everything is more or less even. I make bald-guy jokes now. I tell my friends that I have a robust haircut fund to blow—all the twenty-dollar bills I've saved through the years, all the barbers I've left unemployed. I say, just think of all the hats I could buy, and I point accusingly to Sam's bushy top. *He's so expensive.*

What I tell myself is that I need to look presentable to sit down and write this, so I gather my most professional clothes and lay them in a neat pile on top of the toilet. I grab the Wahl clippers and, like each day that I try to tell more of this story, I pretend that I am going to work.

Just as I've started, I hear the front door open: that tell-tale clunk and click, as the metal apartment door shuts and he bolts the lock. Sam has returned from the gym, and we are once again two big-men-bodies in a tiny apartment. I am trying to claim the bathroom through my silence, through my lack of a greeting. This is my space for the moment. We are still setting rules one year into this work-from-home experiment. Our new rule is that he is to ignore me until I tell him I have finished writing for the day. I can sense him hovering.

He knocks on the bathroom door: "Can I come in?"

"Fine," I say, assuming he really needs to pee, and then I see his sweaty gym clothes and realize that he did not shower at the gym, which means that I am going to have to rush my routine or vacate the bathroom so that he can shower and clean up for his first therapy session, which begins in thirty minutes.

I am annoyed, and I'm not hiding it.

"Lauren's dad died," he says. "He had a heart attack. He wasn't answering the phone, so they had to send someone over. They found him dead."

I am naked, unshaven, unshowered. I decide I cannot process the news this way. I say, very curtly, "I need you to give me a minute."

Sam wilts to the living room, and I close the bathroom door.

Lauren is Sam's best friend; one of mine, too. She's one of our anchors in this megalopolis. We feed her cat when she leaves town. We commiserate over the loneliness of life past thirty-five, how our friends retreat further and further into their children, into their mommies' groups, into the suburbs. We talk a lot about mothers: the friend kind, but also our own. Lauren's mother has been about to die at least a half-dozen times during the last few years. A non-smoker with lung cancer—that cruel joke.

But today's joke is crueler. Death pops up. It springs, it seems, like pop goes the weasel. We hold our breath and Lauren's mother lives another day. Her father goes pop. Her father was not supposed to die today.

I am staring in the mirror trying to figure out why I am angry at Sam. I take far too long trying to figure this out. I debate whether or not I should finish cutting my hair. I put on my robe and open the door, hair half-cut. I try to speak calmly. I say, "What can we do?"

I hate that I ask this. It's the one thing that I have decided has no answer. Or rather, I am frustrated that I don't know the answer.

"I talked to her briefly," he said. His face is white. "Kat's with her now."

"Good," I say, "I'll text Kat and we'll figure out something."

I am afraid to admit that I am jealous. I was so angry that we had to mourn alone, that we were sick with Covid and my mother was dead, that the bagels and pizza that showed up outside the front door came disembodied. There were texts and notes and emails and Facebook messages, but not a person on the couch and hardly a phone call.

Kat, who has known Lauren since their days in college, says to think about "good delivery" and "good food" for the week, and I'm left again thinking of all the starch I ate, how I would have killed for a salad or a piece of fruit (until our taste went).

Sam says he will go to Lauren after work, and we agree with Kat to a tag team of sorts, to make sure that Lauren has enough company, has what she needs to grieve.

Sam looks ten years younger when he is sad. He seems frozen. His best friend's father has died, and his husband is fixated on clipping his nearly bald head.

He turns on the white-noise machine in the bedroom. He prepares for work. I close the bathroom door and return to cutting my hair.

All day I apologize for my actions—that I was so rude when he told me the news. It takes less than the length of a haircut to figure out that I've been a jerk. He has a five- to ten-minute break between each of his patients. "I am sorry for being so grouchy," I say at 11:55, 12:50, 1:57. "I don't know what was wrong with me."

By 2 p.m. I have met my daily word count (this damn thing again) and I head to the gym to work off my stress and shame and Covid weight gain. By chance I see Kat, who has just left Lauren.

She says, "She needs to see people right now."

Kat says she has a key to Lauren's apartment, that Lauren stopped responding to her texts or calls this morning, so Kat walked over and let herself in the front door.

And how did Lauren react to this? She fell into Kat's arms and set to crying.

Kat tells me about the morning, about Lauren, about the dad, about the dying. It's awful. Kat looks genuinely sad. She pauses for a second, and then adds, "You understand."

I come home, relay bits of Kat's update to Sam at 4:55, at 5:55. At 7 p.m., when his workday has ended, Sam makes a giant bowl of chickpea and dill salad, which we believe qualifies as "good food" according to Kat's definition.

I tell Sam that he should probably go alone tonight, that he is one of Lauren's best friends, that I don't want to crowd her right now. He thinks about this, then agrees.

He looks at me with a very serious lip. He asks, "Are you okay? Are you going to be okay?"

"Me? Oh god. I'm okay. Don't worry about me. I am fine. Really. Worry about Lauren tonight. Are you okay?"

He raises an eyebrow, which I think means "Your mother."

He says, "I am just trying to keep everyone that I love alright."

He serves me a bowl of his chickpea salad, which is indeed "good food," and he takes the rest to eat with Lauren.

When he is out of the apartment, I collapse on the couch. I can feel it all coming out.

He checks in every hour or so. I'm fine. She's fine. Everyone's sad.

I make myself a cocktail at 10:30 p.m. As I'm sipping my Manhattan and trying to make sense of this hellhole of a day, it occurs to me that I can't remember the last time I spent an evening alone.

I am sitting in the little park in Brooklyn again. I am holding a note that I wrote to myself. The note is scrawled in my awful handwriting on a sheet of notepad from St. Jude's Children's Research Hospital—a notepad I received this week that came in an envelope along with those tacky, preprinted address labels that nonprofit marketers think will encourage donations. I am fond of the poorly drawn fireflies on the labels, and I hold onto them, pretending that I will someday use them for correspondence, just as I last year held onto the stickers from the World Wildlife Fund. I have never donated to St. Jude's or the World Wildlife Fund, despite their many attempts. The only person I write physical letters to is a mentor whom I hold in high regard but whose success intimidates me, and I am somewhat ashamed to say that I would be too embarrassed to use the stickers with the cartoonish fireflies on a letter sent to this mentor, even though I secretly find the graphics charming.

The note says, "Every leaf was brown and brittle and it died." The *it* here is the tree, the kousa dogwood that, in some sense, contains my mother's ashes. June 16, yesterday, is the date I have written at the top of the note, and is the date that she told me. Teresa called just as I was about to open a tinfoil-wrapped falafel pocket, which was to be my dinner. I was starving, and Sam had just finished his last client for the day, and we were about to watch *Jeopardy!* and eat our falafel. I had not spoken to Teresa in weeks, and part of the reason she was calling was to admonish me for not telling her about my travel plans. I had told her son, my nephew, that I was finally coming home, and he had passed the message on as instructed. I guess I had gotten too distracted to give my sister a proper call. I love her dearly, but the truth is neither of us has been able to have regular calls since the first time my mother cut me off. Everything became irregular then.

I mouthed to him, "Eat." I knew this was going to take a while.

On the phone, Teresa said, "Did I tell you that Mom's tree died?"

No, she had not.

"It was last year, actually. Every leaf was brown and brittle and it died. I thought, Mom and Dad must be down there fighting."

My stomach flips. There's so much news buried in this statement. Had she mixed my father's ashes with my mother's? Was he, too, in this tree?

I said that it was awful about the tree, and no, she hadn't told me, and for a moment, everything I'd thought about my trip home, a trip I would commence in one week, had been thrown for a loop. I did not ask her about my father's ashes then, because the revelation had left me too dumbfounded, certainly too dumbfounded to inquire about the exact contents of the soil surrounding a dead tree. I had been planning this trip for nearly a year—working up the courage to travel during Covid, trying to abide by the strict quarantine restrictions mandated by my job teaching in person. I had been planning this trip, in part, to stand beside that tree, which had stood in for both a funeral and a grave marker. I was to stand by that tree and pay my respects, *respects* being a concept I was still trying to decipher.

"Down there or up there," she said, and it took me a moment to understand her reference. "Wherever."

Sam was eating and watching me talk, and he later said that she must have been saying a lot, because he hadn't seen me that quiet on the phone in a long time, that I barely spoke a word.

And just, perhaps, as I was coming to terms with my dead mother's dead tree, Teresa started again:

"Wellllll—"

The word stretched on and on and up and down. This was her way of transitioning, of telling me that there was a *but more*. When she talks like that, I can see her face so clearly, and how she looks like him, our father. When she goes on like that, she sends me right back to the Moose Club, and I'm a kid sitting on top of the bar listening to my father go on and on as all the drunk old-timers listen appreciatively. She is and always has been my father's daughter.

Well. It turned out that her boyfriend, Richard, who understands plants a little better than she does, gave the tree a chop after everything turned brown, and though it wasn't much more than a stick for the long winter, now it was back, not fully, but with a few dozen leaves.

"Mom must have felt bad," she said, and as I bob my head and take in each new twist in her mythology, I am left only somewhat metaphorically with whiplash.

The note says, "Every leaf was brown and brittle and it died," and here I am sitting in this little pocket park, watching two old men, sitting on opposite benches, taking turns smoking cigarettes and napping, and as I'm looking out at them, and the big, green trees overhead, I'm trying to make sense of my mother and her love of sitting in the park and smoking cigarettes, and a tree that wants to live more than it wants to die. I say to myself, she would like the view from here, and I suspect the old men are beginning to wonder what brings such a young interloper to their little corner of peace.

It's Monday in the little pocket park, and the grounds are littered with the celebrations of the weekend. The park worker, in her green vest, walks by lethargically, picking up stray napkins and paper plates and cups. She wears headphones and is angrily repeating to herself or the person on the other end of her headphones that "This park worker is not picking up these lazy people's trash." The birds are having a day with it—the little bits of leftover food and chicken flesh. There are sparrows and mourning doves, and, because it's the very end of spring, there are beautiful bright mother grackles and brown and dull baby grackles, both hopping in circles while the mother occasionally turns her head to throw food into her child's mouth. I'm watching it all, and I'm listening to the comic mew of the catbird that keeps dancing around my feet. I have decided recently that catbirds are my current favorite bird.

For a whole weekend, I mostly didn't think of her. Sam and I took the train to Asbury Park for his birthday, to the beach, and it was like coming to life again, watching the water and sitting by the pool and then, in the gay light of the Empress Hotel, under the disco ball in the Paradise Lounge, we danced until the bar shut down.

On Sunday afternoon we returned home in time for the whip-lash of Lauren's father's wake. I don't think many of us had been to a wake before. It was Kat's idea, to create a space for Lauren and her brother Danny to remember him, their father who died too early. So we gathered at Danny's apartment and told stories and watched videos and looked at the dozens of photographs of their youth, photographs that were spread lovingly across all the surfaces of the apartment. It was a friends-only affair—a gaggle of thirty- and forty-somethings that felt a little like a party, with wine and weed pens and shared playlists.

I am thinking about how we wail for the dead. I am picturing old women from the old world in headscarves. I can see them throw-ing themselves to the ground, clutching the casket, their pearls, the dirt itself. I was not sure before last night if these portrayals—the ones we see in movies and on television and sometimes in art—were meant to be taken as caricatures or genuine expressions of loss. We alternately laugh at them and feel for them—these sad babushkas and out-of-time matriarchs who cannot imagine living without their eternal husbands or gone-too-soon sons. I am surprised to learn from an Ancestry DNA test that I am supposedly more English than Irish, and we are not too often treated to images of WASPs throwing themselves headfirst into the grave, headfirst into grief.

I had never been to a wake, and I had never before seen someone wail like that. At first it was Danny, Lauren's brother, who said that his father was the second person he had come out to. They were sitting or driving in a car. Danny was nineteen, and he couldn't say it. He said he had something to say, but the thing he had to say, the words themselves, would not come. He said it took his father only three guesses (no, he had not gotten some girl pregnant, which was the first guess, and was, as we learned, the kind of off-color joke his father liked to make). As Danny sat on the couch and related this story to the room, an image of his father frozen on the television screen in the background, he cried out that his father had said "he loved me so much." Those last words came racing out of Danny's mouth and his pitch went up, and then the sobbing came on thick and sudden. It was just a split second and then Lauren cried and then we were all crying in his Brooklyn apartment, some fifteen or twenty of us crammed into the living room, like some Greek chorus or the cast of an avant-garde play about grief. There we were, these nonreligious city dwellers, miming the laying on of hands, like members of an old-timey church.

It was cyclical, like an ebb and flow of the tide I had seen on the Jersey shore in Asbury just earlier that same weekend. Sam and I were sitting on the beach, and we had rented an umbrella. He was so excited to be there, like a kid, and he put the umbrella so close to the waterline, even though it was clear that the tide was coming in. A couple of friends met us, and one said the tide would overtake us soon but not just yet—maybe in an hour or two.

The other friend said we should keep an eye, that when the water overtook the line marked by the beach dwellers in front of us, we should yell, "Breach!" It was so funny, the way she had said it in this exaggerated voice, and we kept watching, and kept asking, "Have we been breached yet?" but the water never quite got there by the time we left to go back to the hotel.

At the wake, we would calm down, and we, the grieving friends, would pat Lauren and Danny and massage their backs and huddle and whisper and then refill our glasses. And Ali, an empathetic actress, kept posing these perfectly framed questions, stirring their memories. One of the questions, which I can't remember, must have hit hard, because Lauren said, "I wish I could have spent more time with him," and "He's the reason I am who I am," and then, *breach!*—the tide had crossed the line—she screamed and cried, as Danny had earlier when his story got to the point, and she ended with such a specific phrase: "He softened me."

I had never heard a person described like that. *He softened me,* as if he were a process and Lauren the result, as if a parent were a kitchen mixer and the child a rough dough in need of kneading. For a moment, I wondered what I hadn't thought of them, my mother and father, about what they had done for me, done to me.

Lauren, a sharp and smart and professional woman, someone I think of as a fighter, as powerful, who for a long time intimidated me, wailed as if she were one of those old-world widows. She screamed and rushed to get the words out: "He softened me," she said twice, and she clasped her hands over her face. As the tears poured down her cheeks and onto the hands of the friends who rushed to her side, I thought that you could see him in her, this man I'd never actually met.

We sat on chairs, on the floor, on all the edges of the sofa, and I chatted with a man who had lost his father a little over a year ago. He said, these things don't go away, not quickly. And another friend had lost his father when he was eight, and, *breach!*, then it came out that I was heading to West Virginia for the first time since she had passed, and for the first time, I think I began to tell people that this trip was for putting certain things to rest. Lauren said to me, through tears, "I'm sorry I wasn't there for you last year," and I said no, you were, and she said, "No I wasn't. Not the way you needed me."

Kat said it was good for Lauren to cry like this, and Sam kept looking at me from across the room, like I was so sad and delicate, and as he looked at me, I continued the slow process of admitting to myself that I really hadn't cried enough and that I really had thrown all of it out when she first hurt me—religion, ritual, the works—all of these things dead to me so long before she died.

We were quiet, and then the emotions would build again, the tide of emotion coming across that line. Something would get him, and Danny would wail his call, and Lauren would wail her response. We stood there as witnesses. It was neither caricature nor maudlin, I decided. This, I could see, was grief—the unfiltered emotion of losing someone who you cared about.

Before we left, I was standing with Sam and Lauren, and I told her what I remembered about shiva. If we were sitting shiva, I said, we would have to rend a piece of her clothing. She asked why, what was the point, and we looked to Sam, who should have known but never remembered any of these Jewish things despite his heritage. I said, I'm sure I have it a little wrong, but it's about grieving, about being so at a loss, that the only reaction is physical, that the tearing of the fabric is a pure expression of loss. Imagine the kind of person who is so bereft they tear their own clothes, I said. I fingered the lapel of her Hawaiian shirt, which she had been wearing in honor of her dad, and I said this is too nice. There were some loose threads on her cut-off-jean shorts, and together we each grabbed a strand and we tore them as best we could.

Sam and I went home, and I said it again, "You don't have to worry about me," but he hadn't been drinking and I had, and his sober eyes said he knew better.

I grabbed one last beer from the fridge and sat on the couch, and we were quiet.

I googled the rules of sitting shiva and the rending of fabric, and I saw that I had missed an important detail. There was something I saw about the location of the tear, how it should be torn, if possible, over the heart.

I finished my beer. We brushed our teeth. For the seventeenth time that day, just before we went to sleep, we said how fun it had been to be away, at the shore.

If the subject of my mother arises, a particularly astute friend I haven't seen for some time will inquire about how I've been doing and respond, Wait, there wasn't a funeral? They'll add, Oh, Covid, of course, and I will say yes, of course, Covid. The circularity of the word helps—the stringing along of the cause and effect, the logic coming all the way round. These days, Covid is the only word that doesn't require further explanation.

I say yes, of course, Covid, but Covid is always only ever part of the answer. I've told this to my students. I've told this to my friends. I scream it at the analysis I read in the *New York Times*. Covid is the filter that lets us see the world as it is. This is a fact I believe more and more each day.

I was sick—so sick and bereft—that I thought I might die. I thought Sam might die, because he's always out there at the bottom of some deep canyon waiting to cushion my fall. He would swallow my grief, let his insides dissolve in the acid of it, and still be holding my hand as his body deflated. How could there be a funeral?

We could not travel. We were sick and then in quarantine and would remain there for the foreseeable future. Her body would decompose, would be burnt, would be no longer the physical figure I needed to see to make sense of her absence. My sisters had seen her face—as a Protestant adherent to open-casket funerals, this to me was what mattered. I was half-tempted, before they took her to the crematory, to make them video me in—to open the drawer, to hold their camera phones over her frozen visage.

They could have held a funeral without me. I would have been heartbroken but understanding. I didn't want to risk infecting anyone. But my sisters said our mother didn't want a funeral. She didn't want a memorial. She wanted to be cremated and forgotten, the little torture box of our old home sold and the small sum of money divided. Just another step in obliterating herself from the earth.

When I looked back over the years, that was the only way I could make sense of it. I had only the vaguest understanding of what it meant to have a death drive—I'd read just bits and pieces of Freud, who I understood to be outdated. Whatever it meant, I was sure that's what she had been doing. She had gone from the young woman in Neale's Drug Store, the smart-dressed young lady whom the owner almost sent to cosmetology school, to the person who rotated through a series of bleach-stained sweat pants and surrounded herself with half-smoked cigarette butts. It wasn't the clothes per se, but the fact that she no longer bothered. At the time of her death, she had more or less one friend who visited her. She sat alone, thinking of my long-dead father (who also had no funeral), of the unseeable glitter of heaven, of the children who'd disappointed her, of the children whom she'd disappointed. By the end she sat each day in an oversized love seat that seemed to swallow her. On one of my last visits, I'd watched her fall over on that love seat—comically, her body just tilted, like the left side of her had been weighed down with a hundred pounds. She was like a silent movie actor, and she bent to the side at an almost perfect right angle, put the side of her head on the throw pillow, and kept her eyes open. What else could she have been looking at save the end?

No one in my family held funerals anymore, it seemed, because we'd spent all our waking hours grieving life.

There is a photo I keep at my writing desk. There is no particular reason I put it there, except that it is a photo of me as a child and when I saw it recently, I thought it might help me remember. It looks to be a three-by-five. It's glossy and developed on Kodak paper. On the back in pencil is my handwriting—large, angular, and awkward as ever. I've written, "Me age 7." There's also a curious piece of masking tape on the back that says just "6" in red ink, and for a moment, I wondered if someone hadn't corrected my age.

The photo was in the time capsule, I realize, the one I made in my fourth-grade classroom and put away. I said I'd wait twenty or twenty-five years to open it, and I kept that promise. Inside the capsule was a collection of ephemera from that point in my childhood. The contents of that capsule have scattered to one memory box or another, but what I can remember placing inside is an X-men comic book, which is what I spent my time reading at that age, and a bouncy ball, which was small and rubbery and the kind you get by popping a quarter into a toy machine. I would say I have no idea why I wanted to leave the bouncy ball in my little time capsule, but that would be a lie. I had hundreds of them during my adolescence. I can still smell the rubber on my fingers, can still feel that rubber disintegrating bit by bit after I'd tossed the ball for the hundredth, then thousandth time. I used to bite those balls— purposefully breaking them in half in my mouth. I'd pull the broken balls out of my mouth and spit out the foamy rubber bits onto our sidewalk or into the grass, and there would be little bits of ball on my fingers and my tongue and on my clothes.

I bought them for a quarter in the toy machines at grocery stores and in the vestibules of restaurants and most frequently at the laundromat with my mother, where I was often the only kid and seemed to have free rein of what felt like a metal and glass castle. I bounced the ball everywhere in that laundromat, even around the woman with the big blonde hair who sat in the back office and also did the wash and fold. This woman would smile and hug me and would sometimes chat with my mother. I believe she was a family friend. I cannot remember her name. I don't know why, but I feel that this memory matters. I puzzle over this *why* for a while. What I arrive at is that my mother, the housecleaner, was calm there, that she felt comfortable around this woman who folded other people's laundry.

The laundromat is gone now, demolished to make way for several neat rows of metal self-storage units. What I have from that time in my life is the time capsule, the bouncy ball, and the creased and folded photograph from when I was seven—item number six in the capsule. In the photograph I am the child I remember, with the same bowl cut I would keep all through elementary school, a pair of blue jeans, and a sweater over a white t-shirt—that layering style that was so popular in the nineties. What surprises me now is the expression of the face, how seriously the boy in the photograph looks at the camera just as the man in the mirror looks back at me in the here and now. I am sitting along the edge of my beloved backyard creek, and judging by the speed and depth of the water and the coat around my body, it looks to be a cold, fall day, not long after a rainstorm. I'm holding one hand in the air, demonstrating something about the water, and my face is so serious—pursed lips, bags under my eyes, chin tilted to the left. I am not sad. I cannot say if I was happy or unhappy. I always say that babies look like little old adults, and here I am, seven, looking like I am telling the history of Weese Street, of Wees Run, the great creek that raised me.

Out of the mouth of babes, or perhaps, out of the minds of babes. I was eight or nine when I made that time capsule, and I sit here now wondering what it was that I wanted to tell myself. X-Men comic books. Bouncy balls. The boy with the serious face.

We can't go back in time, I suppose, but we can touch and taste and see our way back to who we were. Misunderstood mutants and rubber balls for a quarter and the water running so high. My mother in her calming place and my imagination set on a future that I could see so clearly. I imagine the words: *You'll want to know that this was real, that you existed here, in this place. This was your birthright. When the old home has crumbled, you'll still be sitting here on the banks of the mighty creek.*

12

A little over two weeks after we first came down with Covid, Sam and I were declared noninfectious by our doctor. As soon as we got the news, we left our apartment with scarves wrapped around our faces and the intention of making it to Prospect Park. We made it one block, to a bench on Grand Army Plaza. We were out of breath. We were tired, and our lungs and hearts ached. We looked out to the traffic, quieter than we'd ever seen, and we held each other's hands while we wondered aloud what parts of our bodies would be damaged for life.

Healing comes in fits and starts. There are good days and bad days. In a week after that first walk, we could stay out of the apartment for half an hour. We ran our faces through the blooming low branches of the cherry trees at the North Meadow of Prospect Park. We clung to the wrought-iron gates surrounding the Brooklyn Botanic Gardens, angry that we were locked out, that there would be no Sakura Matsuri, no rite of spring. We took deep breaths as it sank in that we were living.

Sometime around those first weeks, my taste started coming back. It was gradual, a surprised delight upon eating a sandwich. Finding those missing tastes felt like the first hit of a cigarette when you've quit smoking for a year. In a month, we were pushing three-mile walks, pushing our tight chests to the limits. We walked three miles, four miles, five miles. We walked the shoreline of the East River and across the Manhattan Bridge. Sometime around three months, we declared ourselves more or less back to normal. That was it, we decided. We were as healed as we were ever going to be.

I have not gone back to my doctor. I keep almost making the appointment. I am sitting on this task. We have moved to a new apartment. I tell myself that the old doctor is less convenient, but I wonder if the truth is that I am scared about what the doctor will find. Sometimes I touch my chest and I imagine my fingers as X-ray cameras. I try to imagine what a damaged lung looks like in black and white, in color. In most cases, our viscera remain hidden. This is probably for good reason.

Each time she struck me down, I could feel my blood and guts spilling out. *She lost it again,* I used to tell my friends, my coworkers, my professors. I'd said it a lot, so much in fact, that I am wondering if that's the anchor—the number of times I uttered that phrase over a glass of wine, on my lunch break, on the telephone, on chat. *She lost it again,* which implied there was a thing to lose, though the *thing* we were fighting for, the *us* in question, became less distinct with each separation.

She lost it in October 2004, in September 2009, in May 2012. There were other times, of course, but those were the big ones—the dates when she decided she could no longer accept some part of me, when she said something so awful that I had no choice but to scream that I'd had enough—again—that I would never forgive her—again—that I would never subject myself to her violence—again.

But she always came back, and I always relented.

She said things like, "Please, Jon. I am your mother. We are a family."

She said things like, "I cried alone every night when you were gone."

She said things like, "I now know that the devil was inside of me."

I couldn't say now the date of each of those rejoinings. She would call me out of the blue—two years of silence and a cell phone vibration. I was never quite sure if I could trust her. I said maybe. I said we'll see. I spent so much time protecting my fragile heart. I could never fully bring myself to believe her. She spoke to me, and as she snuck back into my life, I retreated into some kind of safe blackness. Now I search and search for that place inside of me, for the memories of how she did it, but I find nothing. Just blackness. Somewhere in that blackness I relented each time and said Okay.

She disowned me when I was twenty. She'd spent half a year on the phone telling me I was dying of AIDS, and yet there she is, in the memories and the photographs, at my college graduation. She crept back in. It had been a phone call, certainly. She'd been contrite. But when and how she made her case, why I said yes, I just don't know.

She was there when I moved to New York City. She visited that apartment in Hell's Kitchen, and for a few days I remember thinking we might be alright, that maybe we'd entered a new phase, but then she was gone with a storm of words. She'd seen gay men everywhere. On the streets. In the museums. She spit venom thinking about it. I can still see her face when I kicked her out and sent her to the bus station.

I could make a list of every parting. I could try to put it all on a time line. She disowned me. She came back. She left in a rage. She came back with a whimper. Three times? Four times? Five? I hear years of silence—I search my memories and hear that constant buzz, the sound of static, as I hid in that safe, black space. From my twentieth birthday to my thirty-fifth year, I put on bandage after bandage. And she ripped and ripped and ripped.

I want to ask myself why I ever let her back in. But the question that seems more pressing is how she did it, how she could pull the wool over my weary eyes time and time again. Some days I feel so foolish. Some days I remember to be kind to myself.

After college graduation, Sam and I spent a year teaching English in South Korea. I had never gone abroad, despite my mother's lies to my father about studying in Paris. I told Sam I needed to see the world. And that was what we did. We arrived in Seoul and pretended to be "good friends" so that we could live in the same apartment and teach at the same English school. We traveled to Japan and China and Thailand and Vietnam and Cambodia. I'd never felt so alive.

It was a good year, but there came a point when I once again decided that the difficulty of living in the closet in a conservative society counted for more than the joy of living in and experiencing new cultures. Korea was extraordinarily advanced technologically—advanced in so many ways, really—but its gay-rights movement was struggling to lift off of the ground. When we neared the end of our contract, when we'd refused our school principal's hundredth offer to go with him to church on Sunday mornings, we more or less flipped a coin. It was Boston or New York, New York or San Francisco—the places where we had friends, and, we reasoned, the places we could be out and open. We said good-bye to Korea. We vowed never again to live as just "good friends," and we decided on a whim to move to New York.

We settled in Williamsburg for a year. I got a temp job and then a full-time job, and Sam took his GRE and started sending out applications for psych grad school. In the fall of 2009, he moved to New Jersey and started at Rutgers. For the first time in some five years, we decided to live apart. I was starting my second year of working at a multi-billion-dollar hedge fund in an administrative role, and I didn't want to move to New Jersey. I was the second assistant to one of the head marketing honchos, and I rented an apartment with my high-school friend Mandy in Hell's Kitchen. I'd walk to work, stress out over a dozen business trips I had to plan for the big boss, and then I'd spend the evenings drinking too much wine, listening to Fleetwood Mac on repeat, and smoking cigarettes out my bedroom window. Mandy and I would sit in that window and gawk at the naked man who lived across Forty-Fourth Street and left his curtains open. We'd drink more wine, eat our Chinese takeout, smoke another cigarette. Our apartment was directly across from the fabled Actors Studio (and diagonal from the naked man), and there was never not something to look at. The actors, of course, and the homeless folks and the boys walking hand in hand to and from the bars. My window was my indulgent perch, where I could absorb the wild world of Midtown and try to imagine how I'd fit myself into the chaotic city.

I was juggling a stressful job, having been rejected across the board from creative writing grad school (thirteen applications and thirteen rejections on my first try). And of course, I was still dealing with her. We were *working on things*. We were recovering from the mess of the college years and giving our relationship an honest try. She begged and promised—we could just give it another shot. We would talk on the phone almost weekly, and without Sam there during the week—he would take the train in on Fridays—I think I softened. I let my walls down. It began to feel like my first days in Providence, when she was the one I'd turn to in order to share my awe. The cityscape had changed, but it was all the same.

"My office is on the thirty-fourth floor!" I shouted into my cell phone, a little drunk on Merlot. "I can see the Times Square Ball from my window. You wouldn't believe it—all the skyscrapers here." And it was just like I was eighteen and on my own for the first time again.

My reference point was always home, was always her, was always how far I'd come. I was making $55,000, which in 2009 felt to me like a prince's salary, which was to say large and unearned. I kept thinking of how hard I'd watched my mother scrub floors for just a hair above minimum wage. I told her on the phone, "Tell Dad I kept my promise." The promise had been to work in an office. He'd made me promise to find a job that didn't require me to work with "my hands."

It *was* a large sum of money. I've never lost perspective on this, but I've also come to realize that it was a pittance compared to the millions my boss made, to the six figures the junior bankers made. In segments of a certain Manhattan milieu, some would say it was barely a living wage. I was an assistant—a *second* assistant. Still, I couldn't resist basking in my newfound money, in this tepid grip on a corner office with a view of Times Square and the Hudson River. My first-year bonus was enough to pay off the more than $10,000 in credit card debt I'd accumulated trying to keep up with the rich kids at Brown. My mother kept saying that I'd run the hedge fund one day, and I'd only halfheartedly tell her that this wasn't possible. It was like we'd returned to the myth of my youth, when she'd watched me get straight As, when she'd declared weekly that God had great things in store for me, that I was going to change the world. My conversations with her always bore manic exclamation points.

The hedge fund gave us something to talk about that wasn't Sam, whom she'd rarely bring up. We'd talk and I'd smoke cigarette after cigarette out the bedroom window, and maybe, just before we'd hang up, she'd say, "And how is Sam?" which I suppose was progress, considering she'd spent half of the prior five years trying to get me to agree to never talk about him (*Your rules up there, our rules down here*).

My mother and I were not quite okay, I realize, even though we talked on the phone, even though I mostly held it together at work. I remember sitting in the office during the quiet days leading up to one of the big holidays—Thanksgiving or Christmas—and my boss, the first assistant, asked me my plans. I told her that I would spend it in New York with friends. Not family? she asked. No, I said. And she must have given me her I-can-tell-something's-off eyebrow, because I burst into tears. She called me honey and babe—I was so young and gay that women were always giving me names like that. She handed me a tissue, and I told her a redacted version of my story.

I didn't want to be the kid who cried every time someone mentioned a holiday; I'd been trying so hard to get past the years spent sobbing in my professors' offices. I still believed then that I could fix us. I made a plan for my mother to come stay with me for a few days, and I hoped I could show her that my life—the job, the apartment, the money—added up to some kind of success, to something she could be proud of, to some irrefutable evidence that I was on the right path. She said she was sick and tired of staying at home. Our town, Elkins, and West Virginia in general, were just depressing. The cold. No sun. Her allergies. She agreed to take the Greyhound. She was still too scared to fly.

Since I'd left for college, I'd only seen my mother a handful of times. Each time, something seemed to have left her—her hair became whiter, shorter. Her weight seemed to drip off her. On that trip, when she arrived at the Port Authority Bus Terminal on the evening of September 3, 2009, she stepped off the Greyhound and looked beat, like she'd just finished the biggest cleaning job of her life, like she'd been on hands and knees wiping the marble floors of some coal baron's mansion. She was smiling—despite the twelve-plus hours of sitting in those cramped seats, the three bus transfers. She was smiling, but she also seemed to have deflated.

We walked back to my apartment—a walk that would have taken me all of ten minutes—but it took us nearly half an hour. "My legs are acting up," she said, and we'd walk half a block, lean against a wrought-iron gate or the glass of a storefront, and she'd rub her calves. She said the pain was constant when she walked, that it had been getting worse and worse over the years. And why didn't she go to the doctor, I asked, but she brushed me off and I knew not to press further.

At that moment, I realized just how much we never said to each other on the phone. She never told me about her physical pains, about her money woes, about the troubles with my father. Nor did I tell her that I cried to my boss, that I felt sometimes like a failure, that my job was so stressful at times that I dreamt regularly that my Blackberry work phone would explode in flames, that I would die in my dreams once a week by conflagration. When I saw her like that—weak, nearly crippled—I felt ashamed. I wanted to care for her. I wanted to ease her into a quiet retirement. I wanted to buy her the fabled house on the beach. I kept thinking of how we'd once been inseparable, how I'd rubbed her rough-skinned feet and how she told me over and over that I was the best thing that ever happened to her.

Being around my relatives always triggered some whole-body transformation. My accent would come back. My speech slowed. My shoulders would begin to shrug. And it wasn't just my relatives. At the sight of camouflage, cowboy boots, or a grandmother's poodle perm, I became a yes ma'am, no sir, metaphor-slinging church boy.

My mother and I walked slowly to the apartment. I held her bags, kept one arm around the small of her back. Despite everything that had happened between us, despite the vile things she'd spit in my direction, the night terrors she'd foisted upon me, I told her, "I want to show you a good time."

I was covered in so many calluses, hardened head to toe, but I was still raw underneath, so full of a desire to love her and the world and to make things right. She'd cut me, bruised me, and squeezed me dry. But I remembered her mother's kiss, the hope she'd placed in me, the suffering she'd endured from my father. I thought if I smothered her with love on that trip, I could liberate her mind and body. I just had to show her the joy of the city, the joy of my life, the little pockets of joy that kept me moving forward. She'd spent so much time looking toward the hereafter. I wanted to give her a reason to live in the here and now.

Sam was in New Jersey for part of the trip and came to join us for the second half. We reasoned it was probably best to ease her in. Or maybe he'd felt it was best for his own mental health. When he arrived, she was polite enough in his presence.

We took a lot of cabs, because she couldn't walk. I paid for each ride, because I felt it was my duty. We went to the Metropolitan Museum of Art—she was impressed. We came back to Hell's Kitchen and had dinner on Ninth Avenue—she was less impressed. I watched her watching the scene. I could see the twitching. She held her tongue, so I tried to write it off.

Years later, in one of her fits, she'd cluck, "I know where you lived. I *saw* where you lived." She'd seen the men walking hand in hand. She'd seen the men giving me and Sam the full once over, her body nearly invisible to them.

But she held her tongue until the very end.

It was a Sunday. Sam went home to New Jersey—he had classes on Monday morning and he needed to prepare. My mother was sitting on the couch with me and Mandy, my roommate who had grown up with me back in West Virginia. My mother's bus would come in a few hours, and we were chatting and reminiscing and gossiping about how different our lives were compared to many of our friends back home. Everyone back in West Virginia was already getting married, starting families.

"I'll probably be the last one," Mandy said.

"That's not true," I said. "I'll be the last. I'm not even legally allowed to do it."

My mother had been sitting there, casually listening along, and suddenly her face hardened.

"Do you want to get married?" she shot out. "Do you and Sam want to get married?"

Mandy and I were shocked. The conversation had been light-hearted—but my mother's voice came out as hard and heavy as a lead pipe. I looked to Mandy, unable to speak.

"Whoa," she said. "We were just joking around."

"You and Sam cannot get married," my mother said. "That's disgusting."

"What is your problem?" I screeched out. "Maybe I do want to get married."

It devolved into a shouting match. Before long, I kicked her out of my apartment and told her that she could spend the rest of the day alone waiting for her bus at Port Authority. I told her I would not permit a bigot to stay in my house.

Mandy kindly escorted my mother back to the bus station. My mother would have been lost if she had to go out by herself, but I didn't care.

Just like that, with nothing more than a silly comment between friends, I had surfaced the ugly truth of how my mother felt about my relationship. Or about me. I couldn't see a difference between the two, even if that's how she would have preferred to view the matter.

We stopped talking, despite that brief Pax Romana. I was back to being an orphan. One day, when she became lonely enough, guilty enough, I would be reclaimed. I was beginning to understand that this pattern was the status quo.

13

In the summer of 2011, Sam and I had been together for seven years. We were living in Brooklyn, sharing an apartment with an old friend from college, and I was on summer break after my first year of graduate school. I had finally been accepted to a master's program in creative writing, and I was working on the stories that would form parts of my first book. Sam was deep into his own graduate program, learning the ins and outs of therapy.

We'd set up a small television in our living room, and I'd attached an antenna. We used the TV primarily to watch *Jeopardy!*, and every other commercial at that time seemed to be for one of those national jewelry chains. I'd watch *Jeopardy!* with Sam, and the jewelry commercials would come on, and I'd hold out my hand, wiggle my ring finger, and joke about wanting a diamond. I'd joke to Sam and I'd joke to all my friends, and then I'd have a couple drinks out at the bar, and I'd keep going until I'm pretty sure that everyone began to realize that my shtick wasn't much of a joke at all.

We'd talked about it, even though it wasn't yet legal for people like us. Things had been moving across the country—in Massachusetts, Vermont, California—and it seemed only a matter of time before the laws caught up in New York. We'd talked about how we were committed to each other, about how we couldn't see a future without each other—but Sam had a particular reaction to the word itself, to the institution it represented.

Marriage. He'd say the institution is flawed, the institution is patriarchal, the institution is outdated. I didn't disagree with him—and I still think he's right—but I found myself in that hypocritical situation of wanting to reject a thing but also take part in the thing. It was and wasn't hard to explain. There were practical reasons: Prior to grad school, Sam had been on my company's health insurance, but as my "domestic partner," which meant that we paid taxes on the benefits he received. We'd all heard the horror stories of partners being refused from visiting their sick loved ones at hospitals. We were young—we weren't yet concerned about things like Social Security death benefits and families contesting wills—but we also understood that we would be young for only so long.

There were legal things, and there were other, intangible things. This was harder for me to explain, and so for a long time, we watched *Jeopardy!* and I'd keep sticking my hand out stating my desire for a diamond, and Sam would become increasingly aggravated. "Is this important to you?" he asked directly, more than once, but all I could ever do was stutter something ironic and noncommittal. Yes and no. Maybe. Sometimes. I worried about buying into a life shaped by that much-bandied-about word, heteronormativity. Heteronormativity! As if anything about two men living and sleeping together could ever be heteronormative. Still, it was a fear I had, a fear that came as much from what I thought Sam thought as it did from some version of the queer community that I held in high regard. Sam wasn't exactly an anarchist, but at times I perceived myself as some straight-edge kid in a button-down shirt dating a member of the Ramones. When it came to our political vision, I sometimes felt like Kevin from *The Wonder Years* while he was as forward as David Bowie.

In the background of our increasingly long-term relationship was not just Massachusetts, Vermont, and California, but the very real fight progressing in Albany. Just as our relationship was maturing, as we approached the end of what felt like an endless slog through undergrad then grad school, as we were on the cusp of entering the world as professional adults, the state seemed poised to grow with us. Rumors circulated daily, and it was all I could do to break myself away from the computer for a few minutes. I'd refresh gay blogs and local news sites, and I'd count the votes in the legislature along with the politicos. The New York state senate was Republican controlled then, but support for same-sex marriage was slowly beginning to bridge the political divide.

Sam said he wasn't opposed to the fight for legalization—that to him it was a matter of equality—but his support of the law didn't mean he wanted to take advantage of said law. We'd been to protests in New York. We'd years ago marched on the steps of the Massachusetts State House. I spent hours upon hours wondering if I wanted to marry Sam because it seemed so close to becoming legal or because of something else. The idea of such a commitment seemed to me both beautiful and cowardly. I could imagine Sam arguing, like the Joni Mitchell song I played a little too often, that we didn't need a piece of paper to prove our love. We'd been together for seven years at that point, and we had never needed someone to declare us anything. I knew we didn't need marriage to keep going, but I wanted it—the piece of paper, the recognition from the state, the recognition from our friends. I wanted legitimacy. It was a word that made my face burn.

There was the thing I could not admit: A part of me wanted to get married because in 2011 I'd been fighting with my mother for the better part of a decade, and I was trying to make her see me as exactly that, as legitimate. I could not admit this because I knew that was exactly the wrong reason to get married to someone: marriage as a middle finger, marriage as a fuck-you. I didn't want to start off a new phase of our relationship like that. I knew—had to believe—that marrying Sam would mean something deeper.

I'd been worrying about the same kinds of things since she first disowned me. I worried that Sam stayed with me because he was afraid to leave me alone. I worried that I stayed with him because I was afraid to be alone. These unspoken fears—and they were infinite—had threatened my relationship with Sam from the start. I hated her because of this, because of the complexes she gave me. I would kiss him good-night, and I found myself looking out of the corner of my eye, watching for her dark shadow to hover over and tsk.

In June of 2011, the rumors had reached a fever pitch and had stopped being rumors. On June 15, the New York State Assembly gathered and passed the Marriage Equality Act, and then, after much soul-searching and lobbying, the Republican-controlled State Senate convened in the evening for their vote. It was late on a Friday, and I have always been miserably impatient, miserably nervous on the cusp of big change. I'd decided that I needed to be with others when the vote was taken, that the presence of other bodies might force my nerves to stop buzzing. I was a semiregular at a basement bar called Kettle of Fish in the West Village, which was only a couple of doors down from the Stonewall Inn. I went there by myself, sitting alone at first, until Sam and then my friend and old roommate Mandy joined me. The bar was getting crowded—it wasn't a gay bar, but there were always plenty of gay people there. We were sitting right by the door, and the bartender, who always kept the television on mute (though she mercifully put the closed captioning on during *Jeopardy!*), turned the station to the local news and, for once, turned the music off and the television volume on.

I remember that I'd known all their names—the state senators who might flip and help the bill pass. They voted in alphabetical order. I can't remember who the senator was who turned—there were at least a few according to my memory—but before the roll call had even ended, I knew we had won. I turned to Sam, to the bartender, and said, "Oh my God—it's going to pass. X voted for it. It's going to pass." And it wasn't clear that anyone believed me or understood, but in the minutes following, the vote ended, the senate passed the bill, and the bar and what must have been half of the West Village erupted into screams, tears, and hugs.

Instinctively, we jumped up from the bar—Sam, Mandy, and me—and we ran out onto Christopher Street, right into the road next to Christopher Street Park, which would, five years later, become part of the Stonewall National Monument. It was June, two days before New York's pride parade, and there were rainbows everywhere—on the buildings, on the park fence, and, of course, all over the Stonewall Inn. The street was so packed with bodies that we couldn't move more than ten or twenty feet from the bar's entrance. There were hundreds of people gathering and cheering—soon there were a thousand. Sam was holding my hand, and Mandy was yelling and hooting. We were all so swept up in such a monumental change that there was no room for cynicism or critique. At that moment there weren't radical queers or domestic queers or heteronormative, in-name-only queers. We were present, and we were joyous.

Sam and I kissed there, just outside of the bar, and I can still remember how he looked at me with a deep-eyed stare that seemed so calm in comparison to the frantic energy of the crowd. New York was on the cusp of legalizing same-sex marriage—we awaited only the signature of Governor Andrew Cuomo—and Sam and I were part of something, this big, changing world. He looked at me like the lover I'd always been, but also as something more. It was one of the first nights that I could feel, even if just for a moment, what it was like to be sure that you loved someone truly, genuinely. We were growing up, and the world was changing. I didn't need a ring, but I did want to spend my life with this man.

By the end of the summer of 2011, we had discussed every angle of marriage except for the thing itself—that question—would we do it. It was so strange. We were open about everything. We talked about sex. We talked about the future. We talked about our fears. But the marriage question—it still seemed to vex us.

We'd be home after a night out with friends. We'd come home to our apartment, have a nightcap, loosen up. We'd come close then, but remain purely in the hypothetical. I'd say, "Would you ever want to get married someday?"

Sam would take a sip, eyes rolling back in thought, body sinking with his late-night rye, and say, "I think that someday I might want to do that."

I'd say, "Is this something that you think we should do in the nearish future?"

Sam would say, "It might be something that we should consider."

The woulds, mights, shoulds, and coulds seemed to rule the day. I'd wake up in the morning and realize that we'd moved the conversation exactly one inch forward.

It wasn't that marriage would even change much for us. We'd still be poor students living with our roommate, we were already sharing expenses, and we'd still be finishing the other's sentences. We kept doing that little dance—the late-night conversations, the hypotheticals about hypotheticals—and then we'd put it away for a while.

We lived in Brooklyn then, but we would regularly meet up with my best friend, Mandy, and her long-term boyfriend, Kevin, at this Hell's Kitchen basement bar called The Bull Moose Tavern—now defunct—a half-block from where Mandy and I had once lived together on West Forty-Fourth Street. The Bull Moose was the kind of bar that doesn't exist much in New York anymore—it drew neighborhood locals, gays, Broadway stagehands, and a bevy of blue-collar workers who'd take the late bus back to New Jersey. It was only remarkable for two reasons: one, it was rarely crowded; and two, it had a very nice pool table.

Kevin and Sam got along well because of that table. Kevin had grown up in the Bronx and knew his way around New York fast talking. He was a bit of a pool shark, though a friendly one. Sam, from leafy Maine, had grown up with a pool table in his garage and was just about as solid as Kevin, though less inclined to talk to strangers. They'd team up at doubles, and Mandy and I would sit at the bar and watch them take down most of the challengers, game after game, and the men would keep lining up, writing their names on the board, dropping their quarters on the table. This could go on past midnight—sometimes far past midnight.

I have a love-hate relationship with pool. I actually like to play, but I always find the machismo that creeps up at an open table a bit too much to take in. I would play, and there would always seem to be some asshole making a rude comment or slapping his quarters down a little too hard. Back then, I'd play and miss a shot and then hear my opponent's voice rise to the mock-feminine register or, more overt, a not-so-under-the-breath homophobic jab. Though moments like these were thankfully rare, they happened, and I didn't like it. It all reminded me a bit too much of my childhood, of the bullies on my street and at my school, of my bar-fighting father. I like pool, but I preferred to sit safely with Mandy at the bar.

Kevin could be a shit-talker. He was a brown man from the Bronx who'd often find himself on the tail end of some racist who was pissed that he'd been beaten. Being in any bar with Kevin—and his brown, tattooed skin—was an education in American politesse. It was remarkable that we hadn't ended half our nights back then in fistfights with aggressive strangers.

It was the end of summer, and we were having one of our usual Bull Moose nights. I was with Mandy and Sam and, that night, also our friend Tom. Mandy and I were sitting at the bar; we always took the stools at the corner near the door—and Kevin was winning at the pool table. Maybe Sam was playing doubles with him, or maybe they'd played so many games that Sam had ceded the table to Kevin, who was never one to let go of a streak.

I can't remember the man's face, but Kevin beat him or was in the process of beating him, when this man lost it and slammed down his pool cue a little too loud or whispered under his breath, and then Kevin said excuse me and the man said the racist thing that set Kevin off. They were in each other's faces and they were spitting insults, and then they were shoving each other. The bouncer intervened, and before I could make sense of what was happening, the bouncer threw Kevin out onto the street and, by implication, the rest of us as well. Mandy was yelling for Kevin to calm down and also trying to explain to the bartender and the bouncer that Kevin hadn't been the aggressor. Meanwhile, the racist opponent was also banished to the street and was still going at it with Kevin. Kevin didn't back down, despite our protestations to let it go.

I understand as well as anyone how words can pierce, but I have always had difficulty understanding why men resort to butting heads like animals, how they never seem to back down. We begged him to walk away. We tried to explain that it wasn't worth his energy, that fighting wasn't the solution (still the pacifist), that he didn't want to have the cops called. But he couldn't hear us. He was focused on cutting this idiot down to size. The man had called Kevin something that cut to the quick. And when he'd done so, some defensive scaffolding inside Kevin had broken. There was no stopping what propelled Kevin's fists, what came out of his mouth. They were on the sidewalk and then stumbling into the road, and then Kevin did the thing that he'd been taught to do in situations like these. He pushed and shoved, and as he did so he screamed at the man and called him a *faggot*.

It came out two or three times, and the effect was instantaneous. I was frozen. Mandy begged Kevin to stop, and she was looking from him to us, and I'm sure she didn't have to see our faces to know that a new line had been crossed. There's a special resonance to hearing that word screamed openly by your friend just around the corner from Ninth Avenue, in Hell's Kitchen, in the gayest neighborhood in Manhattan.

"It's okay," I said, and Kevin had begun to cool off, to retreat, and also to apologize to us, but I was already walking away.

"I know you didn't mean that," I said, "but we have to go."

We said good-night. Our friend Tom left. Sam and I marched toward the subway. He looked as hurt as I felt. Mandy and Kevin were right on our heels, every other word a *sorry,* Kevin trying to explain the why of it, that he didn't ever want to use that word. I believed him, and I believed that he'd fought with the man the way he'd been taught, the way that was expected. Mandy, who was from my hometown, used to half-joke that being raised poor in Appalachia and being raised in the Bronx made her and Kevin a perfect match—the people looked different, but the struggles were oddly similar: the poverty, the family dynamics, and, in this case, the kinds of words that men bandied about to protect their egos and maybe even their physical selves. I could see it—the same kind of machismo that Kevin drew upon instinctively was the same kind of chest thumping I'd seen from my neighbors, from my father. To be a man to them meant never to back down, to emasculate your opponent. Kevin had grown up a lot since he was a kid running around the Grand Concourse—he'd talked with us about this extensively—but when he needed to protect himself, he sometimes returned to the lessons he'd learned in his youth.

We'd cooled down by the time we reached the subway, enough to accept apologies, enough to begin to take in the complexity of what had happened to Kevin and to us. We said good-night, and then we went underground. For most of that long, frustrating ride back to Brooklyn, Sam and I hardly spoke. We didn't need to say anything. We both understood.

When we got back to the apartment in Brooklyn, it was well past midnight and our roommate was sleeping. We walked quietly up the staircase to our roof-deck. We could never have afforded such a place on our own, but that was the benefit of splitting rent three ways.

The deck was wooden and slatted; there was nothing special about the deck furniture or the space itself. What was special was the skyline view. I walked right up to the edge—I put my arms on the railing and looked up at the stars slipping out from behind the clouds and then west, over the rows of brownstones and row houses—where just a few yellow and white lights popped through blinds and glass. I looked over to the creeping skyscrapers of downtown Brooklyn, all the way to the bright colossus of Manhattan. The air was August hot, which meant heavy and wet. Sam approached from behind and put his arms around my waist, and for a moment, as the city lights washed over us, I let go of the self that was always on guard.

Kevin had screamed that awful word—the one that seemed to follow us wherever we went—and I didn't hate him, didn't even blame him, really. The man at the pool table had said something just as awful to Kevin, after all. But I was waiting for something, the pain, like a kid who'd stubbed his toe or scraped his knee. I looked out into the night, unsure when or how the pain was going to come but I knew it was going to come. The word made me all at once both numb and vulnerable.

I don't think we even talked about it, how we were shocked or how it hurt or how we understood and would forgive him. All of that was intrinsic, took only a short glance to communicate. The man had said awful things to Kevin. Kevin had reacted. He'd slipped up in the process. We understood all of that. We were hardly surprised.

What Sam said was, "I'm so glad I have you."

What I said was, "And I'm glad I have you."

And out of that awful situation, out of those simple words, came something that was understood between us.

He said, "Do you want to do it?"

And I said, "Yes."

For so long, I've had a hard time articulating why exactly it was that we decided to get married that night, how we were both drawn to think the same thought at the same time. The best I can say is that we realized then, in a world of hate, in strangeness, in happenstance, we had found something that could not be easily replicated.

Mandy took Kevin home, and they soothed each other and kept each other alive. They would also be married in just a few years' time.

As Sam and I kissed, as we held each other and gazed out over the Brooklyn skyline, I think we both realized it would be best not to let this go.

14

I have said it before, and I will say it again. This is the tragedy of my relationship with my mother: It's that in nearly every happy moment—for every joyous milestone—she is there. She was there on the roof, not physically, certainly. But we hardly had finished our embrace, only minutes after realizing what it was that we were doing, that my thoughts turned to the painful fact that I'd have to tell her.

We had been cautiously—yet again—getting closer. After the Hell's Kitchen explosion, when I'd cast her out of my apartment to the Port Authority Bus Terminal over this very subject—that I would hypothetically like to get married to a man someday—it took us more than a year to resume speaking to each other. For a whole year, she had once again gone to her dark place, had once again cried herself to sleep at night. For a whole year, I had fumbled through my work, had tried to cover my slip-ups. I pretended that none of this had taken a toll on me. I pretended to my friends, my coworkers, my boss, and now, again, my professors. And again she had come back—had called and begged forgiveness—had said she was tired of the silence, had asked me to try one more time. What this meant—to accept her back into my life, to agree to try once more—was yet again pulling off the bandages that had been hastily applied and were now being removed far too early. I was not just covered in scars. I was covered in open wounds. We were inching along, existing with something that was slightly less painful than total silence. And now I would have to call her and tell her that it was not a hypothetical. Sam and I were going to get married.

In an email dated December 19, 2009, a West Coast friend was checking in after the Hell's Kitchen blowout and said:

"I'm so sorry to hear that Mom is in a not-talking-to-you place right now. That sucks a lot, Jon. I know that you are incredible at being strong about those things and building a world outside of them, and it makes you brave and adult in ways that I really admire. But still, it sucks hardcore. And I hope hope hope that she will come around again soon."

When my mother came back around—because she always came back around—I would tell people that she had evolved, that she seemed to accept Sam a little more every day. All of this was true, but evolution for her meant the kinds of changes that might have been world shattering for her but felt frustratingly incremental for me. My mother said she could understand our relationship. She said that she could understand that we were together. She had finally told my father the truth, and when he didn't explode, he told me that he had always thought that I was a little *different*, a little *funny*. She said that he said he was happy I was happy (his words were always coming secondhand—he never once called me after I left for college). My mother even said that she cared for Sam. She had even once bought him Christmas presents. Friends, like Mandy, would say they were surprised by how far she had come—and it was true. She had once referred to Sam, in a fit of rage, as my "ugly Jew boyfriend." And so I tried to see her from this perspective, how she could say such horrid things about Sam, and now she could say that she cared for him, that he was "like a son" to her. Everyone was so surprised, but I wasn't convinced.

A mother knows, and the converse is also true. I knew that this announcement would push her beyond her limits. Our peace was more fragile than she let on. I stewed on the idea of telling her for the better part of the next day, but I felt I owed her, that, as my mother, she had the right to know about our engagement before the news became public in other ways, before the word would get back to her (in our small town, even before the age of widespread social media, there was always someone back home who was eager to tell her about my life).

And so the next day, after we'd called Sam's parents, all tears of joy, I went up to the roof, by myself, and I paced back and forth, looking out to the Manhattan skyline and then southwest to the Statue of Liberty. I took a deep breath, and I called her.

I said, "We're getting married."

Her voice was a jagged rock. She said, "Why?"

I wanted to scream.

"Because I love him," I said.

If I could have ridden that cell phone wave across the four hundred miles across the East and Hudson rivers, along the ridge of the Appalachian mountains, all the way to West Virginia, I would have grabbed her by the shoulders and shaken her.

"But why do you have to get married?" she said. "Why marriage?"

"Why did you get married?" I said, though that was not what I cared about. It was a subject that I felt had nothing to do with me or my relationship. In fact, I wanted nothing less in that moment to hear anything about her marriage, her relationship, her skewed views on romance.

She laughed at my question. "I don't know why I got married. You want to know why I got married? I probably shouldn't have gotten married. You don't need marriage."

The tone of her voice could get so caustic. She pummeled through all the same trite phrases. *Anything but marriage. Marriage was pushing this all too far. We had everything else. Why did we have to have marriage?* She just kept going on and on.

"That's a stupid idea," she said. "What do you want me to say? What do you want from me?"

I said, "You're supposed to be happy for me," and I said, "I want my only mother to be at my wedding. I need my family at my wedding."

NO SON OF MINE

And she said, "Wedding? Oh, God. Why are you going to have a wedding?"

I don't know how long we went on like that. I found myself back in a familiar place—tears streaming down my face, heart pumping with anger. The August sun was beating down on my face. A hot wind was blowing up from Flatbush Avenue. I was burning inside and out.

"I wanted you to be happy for me," I said.

She could take any happy moment in my life and turn it into trash.

My friend had emailed, "I know that you are incredible at being strong about those things and building a world outside of them . . ."

For much of the fall, Sam and I looked at wedding venues and hatched preliminary guest lists and debated over the kind of ceremony we'd like to have. During that time, I had also been in touch with a few old friends who were living away from home, and I shared my big news, and we all made plans to meet up back in West Virginia during that Christmas of 2011. Morgan was coming from Shanghai. Tim was coming from Berlin. Mandy and Emily would be in town. Sam and I decided he should stay in Brooklyn—we were worried that things might devolve. I had only spent a handful of holidays back home since my mother and I had started our fighting, and at least half of those visits had in fact turned into brutal shouting matches perfectly timed to ruin the holiday spirit. More than once our fighting had gotten so bad that I'd had to leave West Virginia before Christmas morning (and our cycle of silence had reset all over again).

I took my bus to Pittsburgh with Mandy. We timed our bus to meet up with Morgan, who was flying in. We all arrived on time, and Morgan's brother was waiting to drive us the three hours through the mountains back to our hometown.

Crossing the border into West Virginia has always been transformative for me. It didn't matter which side I came in—from Pennsylvania or Virginia or Maryland—always something would click, and my body would seem to shift. I was no longer a Rhode Islander or a New Yorker or someone who lived in a big city on the coast—I closed my eyes and opened them, and there was the "Wild and Wonderful" sign, the name of the governor, and I was a different person. I had spent so much time trying to shed that skin, but it always came back like that, no matter how much control I had taken of my life and my identity.

Winter in West Virginia can be either beautiful or bleak. The mountains are either white and crystalline or gray and foreboding. That visit definitely began on the gray spectrum. The weather hovered near the fifties, and the trees were brown and there were muddy pockets of snow up and down the hillsides. The pristine blankets of white snow and quaint mountain homes of my memory were nowhere to be found. On that trip, I saw only the trash on the side of the road, the abandoned farmhouses that dotted the interstate, and the poorly kept trailers that erupted from the hills like sores.

Even as I participated in Morgan and Mandy's cheery excitement of returning home at long last, I was also breathing with deep dread over the conversations that awaited me. A month before that trip, Sam and I had signed a contract for a venue in Brooklyn. The wedding would take place on Mother's Day of the coming year. We'd received a 50 percent discount because no one else wanted to hold their wedding on that holiday. We'd joked that our mothers would be there, so who cared?

I wasn't sure that she'd come, and despite all the ups and downs—seven years and counting—I somehow still had it in me to beg her. I couldn't handle the thought that she wouldn't be there. I pictured myself in a room of a hundred people—not a single family member there to support me, as both of my sisters had said they were busy or couldn't make it—and I became mortified. There was some kind of shame embedded in this fear, that somehow I had failed by not working hard enough to keep my family together, or that when Sam's relatives saw me alone, they would see only that part of me—the damaged part, the sullen part. A wedding was a celebration, not a time of pity. I feared that wherever I went, whatever I did, I would always bring this association with sadness.

I wanted her to change, for her to accept me fully. But I had begun to understand that I might never have a perfect relationship with her. The more I realized this, it wasn't so much that I needed her love or her acceptance—it was a new line of logic that was insinuating itself into my consciousness. I needed her to be at my wedding out of convenience. The logic was, *I was tired*. I was tired of having to explain her to so many people in my life. I was beyond tired of having to explain to the hundredth person why I spent holidays alone, why she did what she did. I didn't want to subject Sam and his family to this awkwardness—not on his own wedding day. I was tired of subjecting him to the collateral damage of being in a relationship with me. I was ready to settle for the least worst option. And so, on this trip, I was going to find a way to get her and at least some of my family to come to New York.

Before I came home, we'd talked on the phone, and she'd kept saying, "Why do you need me there?"

I'd said, "A son needs his mother. A child needs his parents at his wedding."

And she'd hesitated. She'd mumbled out, "You don't need me."

We'd gone through variations of this conversation no less than four or five times. There was always a strangeness to her responses. I could always hear the evidence—the meek rattle of an answer. There was a battle being waged in her mind, nothing less than the forces of good versus the forces of evil. She was very conflicted. I was both of these sides—both good and evil—depending on the day, depending on the weather.

After the seven-hour bus to Pittsburgh and then three-plus hours of driving to my hometown, I was dropped off at my old house, which was more or less as I remembered, though with each subsequent visit, I noticed that the size of it seemed to shrink a little more—a shorter roof, a more compact footprint. Even the woods behind the house—we'd called them the woods—now began to appear to me as a mere patch of trees. I could see right through those trees to another house up on the hillside.

She was waiting at the door—she was always waiting at the door when I returned—and she looked like she had been or would soon start crying. This was the moment that could melt me, make me forget the seven years of vicious words and failed promises. I could hear the television out in the living room, where my father was sitting. She said, "Jack, our son is here," and she moved in for a tight hug—and then she did start crying. "I'm so happy you're home."

Again—the same smells, just as I remembered, but maybe more pronounced. There was more cigarette smoke, more wood, more dollar-store potpourri.

The gas stove panel was burning across from the door, and I put my luggage in the corner.

"You didn't tell him yet, did you?" I said.

She said, "Please, don't start this."

And for that day, I let it go. For that day, I played the part of the son that she held in her mind. For that day, I said nice things and told funny stories of living in the city and they told me, like every other visit, how very, very proud they were of me.

It seems impossible for me to explain this now. It seems so absurd that I had ever participated in such a setup. But for years and years and years, she kept my father in the dark about so many aspects of my life. When she'd cast me out that first time, when I didn't show up for that first Christmas, I was "studying abroad in Paris." Even when he found out about me—when my absence had become so pronounced that he could not ignore it any longer—it's unclear to me when exactly she told him that I was in a relationship with Sam. She'd told me that he couldn't handle it, that it would destroy him. She dripped information to him when she thought he was ready. She forbade me from interfering in the process, speaking in the kind of dramatic hyperbole that stopped me dead in my tracks. For a long, long time, I acquiesced with her way of operating.

When I arrived home that December, nothing had changed with her. There I was, back at my home for one last Christmas before my wedding, a ceremony that would take place in five months—I had been engaged for four—and she had not told him, *would not* tell him, that I was getting married.

I imagine an outsider reading this and looking in and asking a simple question: Why didn't you tell him yourself? The answer will not be satisfactory. I don't know how to explain why people follow nonsensical patterns, why people go along with habits that have been ingrained. My mother would not tell my father. My mother told me not to tell my father. I had broken every other rule—had broken the biggest one of all by being gay. I was a liberal living an out, gay life in New York with a man that my father had, in fact, met. He eventually had come to know all of this. How else could I possibly disappoint her or him? How else could I do anything to endanger my relationship to my parents?

The answer will not be satisfactory, because the answer is contradictory. No matter how hard I tried to establish myself as an independent person with an independent will, a person unafraid of illogical, hostile mothers, I still found myself bowing to her at times. We would push one limit—she would claim to accept that I was gay, she would claim to accept that I was in a relationship with Sam, she would claim to accept that we were not breaking up anytime soon—but there was always another boundary. She was my mother, and I believe that in some subconscious sense, all mothers wield some kind of power over their children. Even when I had broken all the rules, even when I did not trust her, did not believe her, when I wasn't even sure that I liked her anymore, a part of me would always be her son, would always be her golden child who aimed to find the balance.

I could have called him up and told him my news. I could have called up each of my relatives—the aunts and uncles I hadn't spoken to in half a decade or longer—and told them that I was living with, sleeping with, and marrying a man. I could have called and told them all that he was Jewish, that he was a good lover, a good listener. I could have called them and told them that I was no longer the boy they remembered in the church choir—that I was no longer testifying in church aisles with my hand raised to the heavens. These are the kinds of false memories that I sometimes fantasize about—the turns not taken—the kind of empowering choices that certain characters make in plays and in movies. And I know such people in real life, too—the ones who are entirely unselfconscious, who exist in technicolor, who have been giving middle fingers to roadblocks, living and otherwise, for the better parts of their lives. I think of these people as the liberated ones.

There is another answer to this question. In the eight years since I had first left home, he'd never once called me. Even during the good times, when my mother and I had patched things up for a year or two, when I'd resume my visits, he'd never picked up the phone and dialed my number. He'd never written me a letter. He'd never driven his pickup truck to Rhode Island or New York. Maybe once every few months, during the good days, my mother would put him on the phone for all of a minute. "Hello, son. Good to hear from you. I love you." And then he was gone, and we wouldn't speak until I returned, haggard and damaged from the war I'd been waging with my mother, and I'd sit on the couch while he watched the news, and even then we wouldn't say much.

The answer is, I did and I didn't care about any of it. What made me angry was the idea that he was an awful father. What made me angry was the idea that he was so out of touch with his only son. What I did not actually care about any longer was our relationship.

Accordingly, I wanted him to know about my wedding not because I needed him to be there. It was rather the idea that a father should know, that to hide this from him was absurd. I couldn't fathom any circumstance in which a father would not know that his son was getting married. I could not fathom telling my friends—telling Sam's family—that my father *did not know* that I was going to get married. I expected his absence. I expected the conversations in which I explained that my father was not someone who had been very present in my life. But for that to work, he needed to know. So I intended, one way or another, to do the thing that my mother could not.

We were sitting on the couch maybe a couple of days before or after Christmas—the timeline remains a little fuzzy to me. The couch that smelled like him, like cigarette smoke and his sweat, a smell that persisted no matter how much my mother cleaned. The couch was a sectional, and he claimed one side and I the other. My mother sat in the kitchen at her table, and she pretended that she could not hear us. She didn't often come into his space, and he didn't often come into hers, but they both kept the volume low on their respective devices—her radio, his television—and they would sit like cats waiting for the other to show a vulnerable moment.

He could say kind things. Maybe that evening—like many other times before—he'd said that he was proud of me. The things he did regularly say to me out on the couch or during the summer on the back porch usually involved my mother, how I should never make the choices they'd made, how she would never be happy with anything, how I should strive to find someone who loved me. And maybe that was why he'd worked up the strength to say to me once or twice that he was happy that I was happy, that he was glad that Sam and I made each other happy—comments that had almost made me feel like we had some kind of connection.

He was a Republican. We'd watch the news and get into minor tiffs about politics. This was our pattern during the visits. They were playful tiffs. Since I'd been a teenager, he'd stopped pushing us into the territory of a true fight. There was no point in taking any of this seriously. Our relationship was zero sum, and accordingly, we'd long ago made our hard boundaries clear.

That evening, something on the news pushed us exactly where I wanted to go.

There must have been something on the television about marriage equality, about New York, about the Supreme Court. Who

–

knows what it was. He made some kind of crude joke about it, and then he said, "You'd never get married to Sam."

And I said, "Oh, wouldn't I?"

And he said, "No, you wouldn't."

And I said, "Well maybe we are going to get married."

And he said, "No, you aren't."

I am not one for flexing my muscles, but every time I sat with him on that couch, every time I watched him with my mother, I pictured myself a gorilla, and I looked at each of us, at his body and mind. I could see him getting old and weak, and I wanted to beat my chest and shove him outside of the circle, to tell him that he was old and irrelevant, that he had caused enough damage for one lifetime, to assume his spot in the recliner.

I said, "Actually, we are. Mom didn't want to tell you."

And he said, "The hell you are."

And we stared each other down, and I didn't look away so that he knew I wasn't joking.

He said, "You are not getting married." And then, "You will not tell my family. My brothers and sister will not find out about this."

There was always some kind of rub. He could accept that Sam and I were in a relationship, but only if we remained discreet, only if we didn't flaunt it. It was family this time, his brothers and his sister—my marriage would rob him of his masculinity, would shame him to probably the only family members he ever cared about.

I told him again that we were getting married, that I didn't care what he thought, what they thought.

He said, "If you get married, I'll come up to New York with a shotgun and shoot you both."

I told him that I looked forward to it. I got up from my seat on that soiled couch, and I walked away, and I didn't say much else to him during that visit.

In five months, I'd walk down the aisle to wed Sam, and I would look left and right and over my shoulder for a gunman.

I wouldn't see my father again for more than four years, and when I did, he'd be sick in a hospital bed on his way to death. They'd bring him home to hospice. They'd place him in my old bedroom. I'd return after that four-year absence, and as he suffered through terminal pains I'd squeeze liquid morphine from the pipette into his mouth. I'd say to him, "You can die now," and I'd think of all the triggers I never pulled.

I think of those remaining days of that visit as the Cold War Christmas. I was tired of explosions. I didn't want to fight. My wedding was coming up, and so I spent the last of my energy on trying to convince my sisters and my mother to attend. Each of them made excuses. Teresa said that her son had an important medical appointment that she couldn't miss. Jackie said she couldn't swing it in New York—not with her anxiety. My mother remained noncommittal. My father and I did not discuss the issue further. I'm sure that in his head he was busy oiling his gun.

No, I wasn't going to fight over this, and I'd said what I had to say. We opened presents under the tree. I kept my mouth shut. I went home, and I slipped back into that other part of my self, of my dual-consciousness.

I was beginning to worry that I had fractured even further. No longer was there the self I reverted to in West Virginia and the self I had created in New York. Now I had to toggle between the self who was ecstatic over my engagement and the one who was depressed by the relentlessness of my family. It wasn't that I hid any of this from Sam—I told him everything that my family had said, that I was upset over my father's threat and my sister's excuses. Nonetheless, there was this intrinsic understanding by which I operated. The understanding was that I needed to pick myself back up, that I could not linger with this negativity. I was to speak the badness once—to Sam, into the air—and I was to march on, again, like I always had. It wasn't fair to him to have to shoulder this burden. If I lingered, I'd let them ruin the best thing in my life. My love with Sam kept me grounded, I reasoned, and I could not let them take away the moment meant to represent the culmination of our journey so far.

So I marched on. With a venue booked, what was left was to decide how to proceed with our ceremony. Between my father's potential violence and my mother's reluctance, I had decided that I couldn't stand the thought of having a traditional, let alone religious, ceremony. Sam was culturally Jewish, and I was a lapsed Christian, more or less a staunch atheist. When I thought of religion and religious ceremonies and symbols, I saw only oppression. Even something as benign as the Jewish tradition of stomping on glass seemed to carry connotations of dogma—the destruction of the temple, a reminder of suffering—and I didn't need such reminders. I'd spent too much of my life suffering because of notions of religious purity. I wanted neither church nor temple at our wedding.

The more we talked about what mattered to us, the more we settled on two notions. What mattered in principle was the legality. What mattered emotionally was sharing this moment with supportive loved ones. We decided that first we would get married legally at city hall—to exercise our rights as citizens. We would then hold a nonlegal ceremony at the venue we'd booked—a true celebration with friends and family. A party.

I'd been talking with Sam about the logistics of the second part, the celebration. Would we walk down the aisle, would we have some sort of officiant? I dwelled on the subject for weeks before settling upon a radical notion. We didn't need anyone to lead our ceremony. What if instead we walked ourselves down the aisle, if we pronounced ourselves married? Hadn't we already decided what we were? Hadn't we spent eight years loving each other without the need for anyone else's permission, recognition, or pronouncement?

It was a little kooky, but I meant it. When I told Sam this plan, he raised an eyebrow. But, like always, he listened to me, and that's why I love him. He listened to my scheme, and before long I'd convinced him to go along with this radical notion: the notion that we—us, our physical bodies, our ideas—were all the authority we needed.

15

She agreed to come. It took more than six months of pleading. When I go back and check my email records, I see that I reserved her hotel room on May 4. The bus tickets were also booked on May 4. I've never been a procrastinator with travel, and though my memory is hazy, the date of the booking strongly suggests that she waited until exactly one week before my wedding—May 11—to confirm that she would attend. I remember she kept saying, *why, why do you need me there,* and I'd said, *it's my wedding, because you're my family.* It felt like we'd had the conversation a hundred times over those six months, and I just kept begging. My dread grew day by day. I kept saying to Sam, *I'm not going to have a single family member at my wedding,* and *I'm going to have to explain to all of your relatives that my family does not approve.* I wasn't sure which aspect was worse. My mother was reluctant to the very end.

We decided that she could spend the first night of her visit at our apartment, to help her acclimate, and for the remainder of the trip, after we'd been married, we'd deposit her in a hotel room in Downtown Brooklyn—the Sheraton, a gleaming high-rise, more expensive than I could probably afford. I wanted to make her feel comfortable, despite how she always made me feel. I wonder now, in part, if I wanted to reward her for agreeing to come, to throw money at a fancy brand, to encourage good behavior. Despite the hassle she'd given me over coming, I also wanted to believe that she was making an effort, that she was coming to support me out of good faith. As much as she'd harmed me, as much as she'd made me lose my mind, I couldn't deny that in the end, she was the only one out of all my family who was showing up. With more than one hundred guests confirmed, she was to be my only family member in attendance.

She arrived at Port Authority and got off the bus—this time the Megabus—and she was neither warm nor cold. I grabbed her luggage, dutiful as always, and attributed her attitude at first to the long trip. She'd been on two different buses for the last ten hours. She looked older and worn, but it was late. I couldn't separate her aging from the bus-ride fatigue—tired or old, I couldn't quite tell. We put her in a cab and brought her to the apartment. We set up a bed-space on the couch in the den—sheets, a pillow, a blanket—and then we told her the plan.

In the morning, we'd wake up and shower and then head to city hall. There was to be a small, informal lunch with her and Sam's family afterward, and then we'd check her into the hotel. We'd have a picnic in Prospect Park on Saturday, a sort of welcome for our friends who'd be coming from out of town. On Sunday, we'd hold the big ceremony—the brunch wedding at the warehouse space in DUMBO, the trendy waterfront neighborhood in Brooklyn.

Before I put her to bed, I said, "It means a lot to me that you're here."

She nodded, and then rolled her head away, facing into the cushion of the couch.

In the wedding album that Sam's mother had made for us, my mother is in exactly two pictures—both on the same page. She's wearing the same outfit—a gray blazer with a white blouse underneath. She has a matching gray skirt and dark sunglasses that hide her eyes. She's smiling in both photos. It's the same smile, the same pose. In one, she's standing outside of our apartment in Park Slope, trees and rows of brownstones behind her. In the other, she's on the corner of Centre and Worth streets, at the edge of that little park across from the Manhattan Marriage Bureau—you can see just a sliver of the graystone Marriage Bureau in the background.

She was there the morning of our city hall wedding. The photos prove it, of course, but I don't need the photos to remember the events of that day. We all woke up and showered. Sam and I shaved, got dressed—I put on a gray suit, and he put on a navy one. I can see him, standing a head taller in front of me—he took his hands and smoothed the shoulders of my suit jacket, then adjusted and smoothed my tie. We both wore silver ties, though they were the slightest bit mismatched.

When Sam's mother arrived, she pinned white roses to our lapels. My mother was dressed and ready in that gray suit—and we took the subway to the Marriage Bureau. I remember holding the pole on the train and thinking, how novel, how urbane, to take the subway to your own wedding. It was Sam, me, my mother, both of his parents, his sister, Rose, and her fiancé, Gif. When we arrived in Manhattan, it had become what seemed like the perfect day for a wedding—the high was seventy and the sun was blinding as it reflected off the stone facade of the Marriage Bureau.

It was the building that was the treat—the building and the people inside of it. The Marriage Bureau is set up like some joyful, art deco version of the DMV. We walked inside to the front desk and grabbed a ticket number. On the wall was a screen that announced the next number in line. There were dozens of couples there, sitting on the retro space-age sofas—think the Jetsons—nestled under the green marble columns, the gilded ceiling, the smooth stone walls. There was something vaguely regal, if not comical, about the space. There were shotgun weddings with bulging brides and gay men in Mickey Mouse hats and old couples of every skin color. There were smart suits and blue jeans and ornate gowns. There were blended families and mothers and grandmothers and great-grandmothers.

The DMV-like screen ticked off the numbers. The room buzzed with anticipation, all of us waiting the forty-five minutes to an hour for our turn in one of the chapels. We'd take turns posing in front of the faux city hall backdrop, a realistic yet miniature-sized photograph installed on the wall of an alcove just off the main waiting area. We tried to peek into the chapels in between the short ceremonies. There'd be periodic hoops and hollers, as couple after couple exited the hall, hand in hand, photographers or amateurs with camera phones trailing.

Sam's mother kept mentioning how wonderful the scene was—she seemed truly in awe of this spread of New York, seemed to understand now why it had been so important for us to hold our official wedding here. She kept hugging us and taking photographs and cheering us on, and even as nervous as I was, it was hard not to feel buoyed by her energy, by the quiet, wet eyes of Sam's father, and of course, by the wide smiles of the other couples.

Sam and I stayed close to each other, waiting, taking in as much of the room and the people as possible—I'd been told that I wouldn't remember any of my wedding day, that the events of such a time are too frantic. And perhaps I wouldn't have remembered much of that day, if it wasn't for what would happen later. I would periodically steal glimpses at my mother. Our spirits were all up, up, up, and yet I could see her beginning to retreat. I could feel the thing turning inside of her—the thing she had promised was no more, the thing she had promised she'd cast away. She would stand in a corner, then sit on a chair. It seemed that wherever she went, she stole the glow from the bright windows, from the warm stone. She was antireflective. She turned the light into a cold, hard void.

I could only look at her in glances. I was with my fiancé—his doting mother, his sensitive father who was ready to cry on a dime—I didn't need to engage with her, with these old games. This was our day—mine and Sam's—not hers, and I couldn't let her rob me of this. So I clutched Sam's hands. I smiled nervously for photos. We watched the screen tick, tick, tick up, and we waited for our number to be called.

The chapel was small, but not tiny. There were two of them, across the hall from each other. We were assigned to the one on the left. There was a wooden dais up front, a couch, some stacked chairs along the edge of the carpeted floor. We walked in, and Sam's mother and father, his sister and boyfriend, and my mother followed. The clerk was a middle-aged woman—round face, trim cut, all smiles. She greeted us with a classic New York rasp that put me at ease. She explained the procedure—it would not be a long one—and we told her our only quirk, which was that we would not be exchanging rings.

Marriage was a compromise, and for Sam, at the time, a ring felt too much—for one, he didn't like to wear jewelry, and two, his own parents had given up wearing them long ago. It had been enough to get him to buy into this institution in the first place. I wasn't going to push it.

No matter. We weren't the first who hadn't exchanged rings. What mattered was all around. What mattered was the family that surrounded me, was the state of New York, was the government and the people and the promise of living with dignity. I was twenty-seven years old the day we got married. Sam was just shy of twenty-nine. I'd spent the better part of my life listening to people bandy about words like "sin" and "abomination" and "unnatural." To be surrounded by our family, by this officiant, who saw us as partners, as lovers, as the whole, honest package—standing in that room and holding Sam's hand allowed me to bury the preachers of my youth, the loudmouth neighbors, the crass bullies. We were standing on the soft carpet of the chapel, and I pictured them locked in cages under the floor, banging to be let out. What was good, what was pure, rose to the surface. I could see that when I looked around the room.

I tried not to watch her. She stood in the back away from Sam's family, away from us—her hands clutched her purse. She looked downward, mum. I promised myself that I'd keep my focus where it needed to be.

The officiant aligned us at the front, facing each other. I looked from the officiant to Sam. I tried to lock in on his brown eyes. We held our hands across the gap, and I could feel every twitch in his muscles—it was difficult to remain steady.

She walked us through the vows—the *I dos,* the promises—with a voice I could never forget. She spoke deep, with warm gravitas. She was a civil servant, and she took her job seriously, which meant that she took us seriously. She spoke with the highs and lows and waves of an old-timey orator. When she neared the end, when we were just on the cusp of being declared, I remember the delight

I felt as she raised her head, raised her hands from the dais, as if she were going to bang a gavel. She nearly shouted the words, "By the powers of the state of New York, I now pronounce you *married*." As we prepared to kiss, I thought of that wondrous turn—not church, not God, not husband, not wife. Just *married* and *married by the state of New York*.

Sam's eyes were moist, like his father's, and we leaned in to close the gap, to kiss, to the cheers from the room—and it was all cheers, and a hoot or two by my sister-in-law Rose and her boyfriend Gif. I was kissing my husband. *My husband*. We were married, in the eyes of the state, legally.

I will never forget that.

What I also will never forget: As I kissed him, as I took in his face, I also caught a split-second glimpse of the room—of the faces that watched us. And there she was, in the back. Just as I glanced—in that half-a-second that I looked away from *my husband*—she turned her head away. As Sam and I leaned in, she jerked her head around and looked down and to her right, to the floor, as far away from us as she could in that small room.

I grabbed Sam's head tighter. I kissed him harder. I smiled and I smiled and I smiled.

I would not let her ruin this. I would not let her ruin us.

We opted for a taxi back to Brooklyn. In the car, Sam leaned over and whispered. "What's going on?" he asked.

"We'll talk later," I said, and I squeezed his hand. I squeezed his hand so much that day he must have been sore by the end of the night.

I kept smiling. What I felt really was an overwhelming joy. I was joyful, ecstatic, and full of rage. I could be all those things at once.

What Sam needed to see was joy, so that's what I focused on, that's how I tried to wear my face.

We made plans to meet up for a late lunch in Park Slope. We stopped at home, but only briefly—we left the suit jackets behind, took the ties off. I bit my tongue. I dragged her out the door and down the block.

We were all there—Sam, his parents, his sister and her boyfriend, my mother. We decided to have something informal. It was a sandwich and french fry place that no longer exists. They seated us on the back patio at a big table under an umbrella.

We ordered, we laughed, we toasted. We sat there for an hour, eating and drinking and recounting the morning. I was tired, running on what was left of the energy from the Marriage Bureau.

She barely touched her food. She hardly said a word to anyone. Sam's family of course noticed—we'd discuss her later. But they kept smiling, kept laughing. And I ignored her the best I could.

They paid the bill. One last toast. I kissed them good-bye. I told them we'd handle getting my mom to her hotel. And then Sam, my mother, and I walked back to our apartment.

Our apartment then was on the top floor, the fourth. Her leg had been bothering her for years, getting worse. Normally I would follow behind her and wait with her at each flight of stairs, but that day Sam and I mounted the three flights of steps in just a few seconds. I stood at the top with the door open. Sam watched me. I said, "She turned her head when we kissed."

I watched as she climbed a few stairs, and then stopped to rub the pain from her leg. She was still wearing her gray skirt suit. It took her at least five minutes to make it to the top. I held open the door for her, and then I followed her inside into the kitchen. I slammed the door shut, threw my tote bag onto the floor. I couldn't contain myself for a moment longer.

"What do you want to say?" I said. "What is your problem?"

"Nothing," she said.

Sam was watching from the far side of the room—watching to mediate or help, I wasn't sure. I knew that he was as tired of these games as I was. This was supposed to have ended. At the very least, today should have marked a day when we became free of such things.

"Spit it out," I said. "I know you want to say something. Say it."

I was vicious—using the kind of tone that she'd used on me, that she'd used with my father.

She just kept shaking her head.

"Say it," I said.

"Let it go," she said.

"Say it," I said.

"You don't want me to say what I'm thinking," she said. "Let it go. I'm here. What else do you want?"

And then I lost it. A barrage of curses, banging my fist on the couch, tears. "I saw you turn your head when we kissed," I said. "We disgusted you. We disgust you."

She was shaking her head. Her body seemed to shake with the dissonance. She was murmuring, "Stop it, stop it," and it looked like she was about to cry too.

But I'd had enough.

"What is your problem?" I screamed. "Why can't you be happy for me?"

And then I screamed some combination of Fuck you, Fuck you, Fuck you, Get the fuck out of my house, Stay the fuck away from me, Leave me the fuck alone, My fucking wedding day, and then I pushed her out the door. I didn't care where she went. She was gone. She had to be gone.

We paced the apartment. I cried and screamed and wailed and Sam hugged me. He tried to comfort me, but he was also so hurt, so full of rage. This kind of thing didn't happen. This kind of thing did not happen on a person's wedding day. My mother was a loose cannon. My mother was a demon. My mother was nothing less than a terrorist.

He hugged me, and we sat cross-legged on our antique green sofa with the hard bottom, and we looked at each other face to face, eye to eye, holding each other, some sodden version of the scene that had played out at the Manhattan Marriage Bureau only a few hours earlier.

"I love you," I said, "more than anything."

I had to speak that—I had to say it over and over again to expel her presence, the words like a ritual burning. Sam and I would kiss, and I'd bury my head in his chest, his white dress shirt soaked through with my tears. It was the only thing in my field of vision: Strands of his dark chest hair pressed against the wet fabric of his cotton-blend shirt.

"I love you," I said. "I love you so, so much."

Sam was my husband. We were married—newlyweds. We should have had strings and cans trailing his beat-up car. This was to have been our moment of bliss.

He'd say, "Fuck," and he'd stand up, and we'd both be pacing, looking out the windows onto Saint Marks Avenue, down the side-walk to the corner of Fifth. "Goddamn it," he'd say, trying to find a place for the kinds of emotions that don't have a name.

"I hate her," I said. "I hope I never see her again."

And as we sat there for the next hour—crying, wailing, lamenting—the seed was planted. I was married, and I was done with all of it. I began to let myself see and feel what that kind of life would feel like, a life in which she did not exist.

The guilt kicked in. It wasn't a guilt that we'd done anything wrong. It was the guilt that I always had—that I was the only adult in my family, that my mother was immature and incapable of taking care of herself. I worried that she'd take a wrong turn. I worried that she'd try to cross the street with her slow legs and get hit by a bus. I worried that she'd get lost and never find her way home. We'd left her roaming the streets outside of our apartment.

"This is the last thing I'll ever do for her," I said. "But we have to find her."

She had no idea where she was. She had no sense of direction, no smartphone. She was a stubborn old lady from a small town, and I could picture her fight-or-flight instincts kicking in. I could just see her, so confused and angry, cursing out strangers on the sidewalk. She had nothing to lose.

We agreed to go out and get her. Sam still had a car then, the one he used to commute to grad school in New Jersey. We'd drive the streets and find her and pick her up and drop her off at the hotel that I'd booked and paid for.

I had imagined that we'd have to drive up and down the streets, cruising block by block, calling her name as if we'd lost a dog. In fact, we didn't have to look far. She was only a half block down the street, standing on the corner against the wall of a Thai restaurant. It was pitiful. She must have been standing there for the better part of an hour.

"You're going to get in Sam's car," I said, "and we're going to drop you off at your hotel."

She said nothing, but she didn't protest.

She hobbled into his old, red Toyota Corolla. She seethed in the back seat, while we glared from the front. The drive couldn't have been more than a mile, but the traffic on Flatbush Avenue was thick and slow.

Sam looked at her in the rearview mirror.

"What is wrong with you?" he screamed. "You're an awful person."

I'd never heard Sam so angry. I'd never heard him talk like that to her. He'd always walked on eggshells, had always, out of respect and courtesy, followed my lead through the labyrinth that was my relationship with her.

Her eyes narrowed. You could see the words forming, almost bubbling up from her chest. She seemed almost to growl. "You boys need to make right with your maker."

I couldn't believe that she'd come back to this again—I was in the front seat, stealing glances at her from the passenger-side mirror, shaking my head in disgust. In the past, I would have yelled back, would have argued the point. But I think I was entirely defeated— after so many years of back and forth, I'd finally settled into admitting that she was rotten to the core. There was nothing to be done. I'd had a jade plant once that had suffered root rot, and I watched as the trunk shrank in on itself—became hollow, so that you could squeeze what had been hard bark and feel the squish of the insides turning to mush. Before long, there was nothing left on that tree but the sad, collapsed skin of the bark.

It was Sam who surprised me. He banged his hands on the wheel or the dashboard. "No!" Sam screamed. "Shut up. Just shut the fuck up."

And every time she tried to interrupt—every block or so as we crawled down Flatbush Avenue—she'd try to say something foul, and Sam would scream right back at her. "Shut up. Just shut up."

I was grateful that he provided me the space to just be silent. My battle with her had always been tête-à-tête. I had never needed him so much.

We pulled up to the Sheraton. I took her luggage out of the trunk. I put it on the ground in front of me. I pointed to the hotel.

"Leave us alone," I said.

I watched her walk across the narrow road of Duffield Street. She opened the glass doors and stepped into the hotel, her face a mix of indignation and sorrow.

Sam and I idled in the car, and I cried as he held me the best he could from his spot in the driver's seat, his seat belt still on. We didn't say anything. I think I was coming out of shock.

We sat in the car collecting ourselves, trying to make sense of what had just happened. My phone rang. It was a local number. I didn't pick it up, and then it rang again, twice, three, four times.

It was the Sheraton front desk. The reservation was in my name, but I hadn't put down a credit card authorization form. They asked if I wouldn't mind faxing one over, that they couldn't give her the keys to the room until I provided my signature.

I got out of the car, and walked across the street into the hotel. She was sitting in a chair in the lobby, watching me. I signed the form. Before I walked out the door, I gave her one last look. I did not say good-bye.

We drove home. I hoped that was the last thing I'd ever do for her.

———

Of course it wasn't the last thing I'd do for her. My mother called my sisters and said that she wanted to leave. I had been the one to book the bus tickets, so I would have to be the one to change them. My family was too Internet illiterate at the time to find any kind of work-around, and neither of my sisters seemed to understand the gravity of what she had done to me, or at least they didn't act like that on the telephone.

I said, "She turned her head when we kissed. On my wedding day. She ruined my wedding." I told them this, and still, they said I needed to change her bus tickets.

On Saturday, the day after my city hall wedding, I would have a huge picnic in Prospect Park as a welcome to the hundred guests who would later in the weekend attend our brunch ceremony at the warehouse venue in DUMBO. I would smile and drink wine and beer and eat picnic foods with friends I hadn't seen in years—friends from college, from my childhood. I'd meet friends and family members of Sam, some of them for the first time, and I'd run around to ten different picnic blankets and schmooze and smile and drink and relive the first twenty-seven years of my life with the people who'd made it worth living.

After that picnic, I returned home and sat down in our apartment. I called the 800 number for Greyhound customer service, and I changed her bus ticket to depart as soon as possible. I sat at my computer and typed up detailed instructions and emailed them to my sister Teresa.

My sisters, I later learned, had told my mother to close her eyes. They'd told her that if she felt like she was going to explode, that if she couldn't handle watching our ceremony, all she had to do was close her eyes.

In the wedding album that Sam's mom made for us, I am smiling in every single one of the photographs. I am smiling at the Marriage Bureau. I am smiling in the park. I am lying back in the grass, sitting in camp chairs, spread across the picnic blankets. In the photos in the park, I'm wearing a pair of shorts and a black-and-white striped shirt—the kind that I associate with French people in the summer—and I look carefree and happy and my eyes are wide open.

My sisters told my mother, "You don't have to look," and she didn't.

I told Sam over and over that weekend that I would not let her ruin this—I would not let her ruin our wedding weekend.

There were seventy-two hours of events, seventy-two hours of extremes. I'd kissed Sam once at city hall, he'd held my quaking body in the quiet moments, and he'd kept his own chin up, pointed forward. I'd cast my mother out—I hoped for the last time—and I began to imagine that new life with the man whom I'd legally wed. All that was left was the final celebration, where'd we walk down the aisle in front of our friends and Sam's family—now my family—and publicly share our love.

He'd told me that was what mattered to him. No, he didn't really believe in the institution of marriage, but he believed in sharing our love openly with the people who had always been there. If I had become fixated on being recognized by our state, by our government, the Sunday ceremony was what Sam considered our real wedding.

There was no wedding party—no best men or maids of honor. There was us, and there were guests. We would get married, and a few friends would give toasts at the reception. The wedding was all of us—the bodies filling the chairs and the floor of the old warehouse.

The venue was called ReBar then—it was billed as a restaurant, a cinema, and a wedding space for nontraditional couples—edgy brides, artists, queer kids. It wasn't really that edgy, but the weathered brick walls and the faded wood floors gave it a certain charm, a certain industrial feel that people associate with parts of Brooklyn. Sam and I got dressed in the morning—in the good suits, the ones we bought new, that we thought we might later use for job interviews—and Sam's family and the photographer followed us from our apartment, to the venue, up the elevator, to the roof. The roof itself was nothing special, per se—that same silver membrane used to cover seemingly all of the city's roofs—but the view was stunning. Just at the edge of the building was the rise of the Manhattan Bridge, the sounds of cars and the Q and N and D trains drowning out our voices.

I had broken my front tooth when I was a child, and though it had been repaired, it still showed black from the screw that held it together. I was terrible at smiling naturally, at taking photos. The photographer kept trying everything—he kept saying, "Jump! Jump!" to jar me out of my awkwardness. And Sam and I would hold hands and flowers and we'd jump, jump on the roof, and he caught a few good ones of us like that, where I'm unselfconscious, with the Manhattan bridge looming but stable behind us.

I was happy. I really was. I keep telling myself that, and it's not a lie, but it was hard to believe it. I felt that no one would trust me when I said it.

My mother wasn't at my own wedding. I didn't have a single relative in the audience. I had Sam, though, and I had my friends—my real family—and that was the whole point. I was happy.

Inside, a hundred people gathered and sat on the folding chairs. It was a brunch wedding, and afterward there would be copious food and drinks, and we were too young to be moderate about anything, so half my friends would be on the verge of collapse before evening.

I was happy because they were there, and for once I allowed myself to be happy that she wasn't.

That was the thinking I had to commit to. Her absence was not a detriment, but a bonus. This was a beginning, a fresh start. I'd tried for years to let her into my life, to let her into my relationship with Sam, to give her space to be a good mother. Rotten, like the jade tree that I'd overwatered, she was pulp on the inside, black innards, unsalvageable. I was free of her. I was happy.

My oldest friend gave me a shot of whiskey before I walked down the aisle. Everyone was smiling.

I didn't need her anymore. I didn't need to waste my time or my energy or my emotional capacity. I needed the man in the navy suit.

He asked me if I was ready. We weren't hiding from each other. We were not sequestered. I said yes.

We walked down the aisle together, arm and arm. We joined in marriage just as we'd been before marriage—by supporting each other's step, by keeping the other upright.

I would have collapsed that weekend if he hadn't been there, if he hadn't told me so much that he loved me, that none of this mattered, that we were what mattered. And because he was there holding me, steadying me, despite all that she had done that weekend and the weekends before, I have allowed myself to admit that even though I was hurting, that a part of me was ashamed that I had no blood family there in attendance, I was also truly and genuinely happy.

Here's what I want to take away from that weekend:

The night of our wedding, after all the celebrations have ended, we head to our room at the Intercontinental on West Forty-Fourth Street. We're on a high floor—something in the teens—and we have a view north over Times Square. The neon burns over the streets as Sam stands behind me, his arms wrapped around my stomach, my arms entwined in his. We are drunk but aware, pressed against that wide open glass. It's the two of us. I feel a bit of poetry in the scene. *My husband holds me naked in the window.*

What we can't see is my old apartment—my first apartment in Manhattan—just one block west toward the Hudson but out of view. Four-nineteen. With enough time, all my New York memories will revolve around numbers, around addresses. What I don't think about is my mother, who in that apartment unleashed blasphemies when I suggested offhandedly that I might someday like to get married. We cannot see the apartment or the Port Authority where she marched from four-nineteen to catch her bus back to West Virginia. She will, in fact, depart from the Port Authority in the morning, once again in a fit of rage and sadness. She may even be marching there now, angry at the word marriage, even as we bathe in this newness, as we look out over the city, as my husband holds me naked in the window.

Marrying Sam is like starting anew. It has not occurred to me why I have needed this. It has not occurred to me that by exchanging vows with him, by making promises, by declaring our love, we are becoming something different, have already transformed. The sense creeps, first through my eyes, as the lights of the high-rises reflect back their story, and then through my arms, as the touch of his skin reveals this new truth. We are in a new kind of love, I think, as my husband holds me naked in the window. We are in the kind of love that wraps and swirls. My worries about her recede. He is my family now.

There have been a few moments in my life when the stress of the world completely disappeared, when my body felt at ease. The first was when I quit my job at the hedge fund, the one that gave me nightmares about Blackberry phones exploding in my pocket. I had been accepted into grad school. I was going to become a writer. So I gave my notice, and I said good-bye to my coworkers. Sam and I ran away to celebrate. We spent two weeks in Seattle and Vancouver, driving across Vancouver Island, ferrying back to Olympic National Park. We camped under those moss-addled trees, and though we were in a rainforest, it didn't rain at all until the last day of our trip. We came home, and I told him I had never felt so at ease before—like a decade had been lifted from my body.

The night of my wedding we are too drunk and tired to have sex. We laugh about it, as we sink into the hotel mattress, as we hold each other and recount the day's events. There is nothing else waiting for us on the other side tomorrow. It is only me and him, a hot breakfast at a diner, a walk through Central Park.

We wake up too early, and our heads are throbbing from yesterday's prosecco. We kiss, we roll in the sheets to hide from the pain of the hangover. We drink water and brush our teeth. We go back to the window and look out at the glass and metal city turned golden orange from the morning light. If we were standing down on the sidewalk on West Forty-Fourth Street, we would see an image of two men, one a head taller, standing naked in the window. We might say that they were happy, in love, full of wanderlust. What I can say is that we are gazing out at the world, and what we see is a reflection, is clarity.

We get dressed. We leave our suitcases in the lobby. We will go home to Brooklyn tonight, but first we stroll Ninth Avenue, hand in hand. "You are my husband," I say in a hundred different ways. "And you are my husband," he says. We try the word on, and it fits. We wear the word like new clothes.

PART THREE

16

My wedding marked the penultimate phase of my relationship with my mother. We passed another four years of silence. I was twenty-eight years old, married, living in Brooklyn with my husband and, for the first year of marriage, with our old roommate. In a way, my wedding day was like going back eight years in time to when I was twenty, back when she had dismissed me the first time. Then, I was scared and nearly alone, unsure of what awaited. The cut had felt fresh and searing, but I could see that inside me was real blood, pumping hard and fast. By cutting me off back then, by cutting me open, she had allowed me to see a version of myself that had been hidden. And here again, on my wedding day, she had swung her ax, left another wound, and though I was bleeding, I could see that she had finally stripped what protective armor was left. When I looked in the mirror—when we brushed our teeth together before bed, when I caught a glimpse of myself standing next to my Sam—I knew that her absence created the possibility of a true liberation. In this partnership with this man whom I loved, in this partnership without the weight of her heaviness on my shoulders, I could create the life that had always been my birthright.

I had betrothed myself to Sam, and when I'd sent her away, I said never again. I kept saying that to myself in those first few weeks. Never again will she tell me hateful things. Never again will she ruin my day. Never again will I deny myself happiness because of her. There was a manic quality to those first weeks after marriage—to my voice, to my carriage, to the way I repeated these promises—but this mantra saved me.

We spent four years in silence, four years apart, and in her absence, in the company of a man who was now my husband, I became a kind of person that I never would have thought possible. My shoulders became taller. My laugh became louder. When I paused and took note, I heard echoes of the unselfconscious child— the one who had been happy before the world applied its oppressive diktats. At first this made me angry. She had, in a sense, stolen years of my life. She had almost consumed me in more ways than one. But then Sam would grab my hand. He would say something simple like "I love you" or "You seem happy" or "We've come so far."

And it wasn't just Sam. The world seemed to perceive me differently. I had gone nearly bald by thirty. I had wrinkles from chain-smoking cigarettes. What was left of my hair was turning silver. New acquaintances often thought I was a decade older than my age. But after marriage, after she was out of my life and I allowed myself to accept this fact, something switched. My hard face softened. My blue eyes turned brighter and less gray. When I walked down the streets of the East Village and Hell's Kitchen, I noticed men's eyes following me to the corner. I was visible. I was present.

I was turning the corner on thirty, and I began to see a beautiful contradiction: I had lost so much, sure, but I still had so much life left to live. I think I began to flourish then.

This is how four years pass without her in my life. After the wedding, I am an adjunct professor of English Composition while Sam is finishing his doctorate in psychology. We quickly go broke, because adjuncting is not a living wage anywhere, let alone New York City, and Sam is a student. I say, I'll quit my job for you, even though I love teaching. I'll go back to being an executive assistant. I'll do the corporate thing now, and when I'm ready to be a writer again, when I'm ready to chase my art, you can support me. He says that I don't have to do this, but I know that I do. I say, this is what a partnership is, this is what it means to look out for your family.

I slip back into my old, corporate self. I work at first for a high-powered Frenchwoman, scheduling her hundreds of meetings and hundreds of flights and working some days from eight to eight, typing reports and editing her documents. I am thankful that this company pays overtime, which is not common for people in my position. I hear that the Frenchwoman has a certain reputation at our company, and she lives up to this rumor. She makes me cry within a month. My coworkers hear us screaming at each other, and then they watch me storm out toward the elevator. The head of administration calls me and says, "Please don't quit. You are the only one who can work with her." She is not my mother, and at first I make excuses for her all the same. I say, "It's a company full of men. Women of her generation . . ." but then I catch myself. I tell Sam, "I think I'm done with situations like this," and he agrees. He says, "I know when you're happy," and after a year, I decide to take a pay cut and move to a place where I can breathe. I give her more than two weeks' notice because I feel that it's the right thing to do. When she hears the news, she slams her office door in my face. She refuses to talk to me, and on my last day, I leave the office without saying good-bye.

When I get home that day, I am ecstatic to be gone, but also infuriated. I tell Sam, it's just like back in high school. Remember the story I told you about the Iraq War? And of course he remembers, because we've been together for almost a decade, and he knows all my stories by heart.

It was the eve of the invasion. It was fall 2002 or winter of 2003— back when Bush and Cheney were making their cases, when the writing was on the wall about what our country was about to do. I was a senior in high school, and I told my father, an army veteran and a Republican, that I opposed the war, that I opposed all wars, that I was thinking about getting on a bus and heading to Washington to join the protests.

He said, "You're what? Go to your room."

His face had turned tomato red. I was eighteen years old, and I almost laughed at his attempt at discipline, but I went to my room anyway because we were clearly not going to be able to have a conversation about any of this.

I went inside, closed my door, and screamed into my pillow. It couldn't have been more than a minute before I heard his feet thump, thump, thump across the wooden planks of the dining room. He swung open my bedroom door, just enough to stick his head in. "You're what?" he repeated.

"I'm antiwar," I said.

"No, you're not," he said, and then he slammed the door and thumped away.

And then thumping grew louder, and the door opened again. "You're what?"

It was like a sitcom. He must have repeated this process four or five times. Thump, thump, thump. *You're what?* Thump, thump, thump. *No, you're not.* Thump, thump, thump. *No son of mine . . .*

I didn't really care. My father was a lost cause to me politically. I never expected us to see eye to eye. I didn't invest too many emotions into his opinions. What got me was her.

My mother was a registered Democrat. She told me once that she didn't vote in elections because my father had convinced her that by voting, she would cancel out his vote, and what was the point in any of that? And so my mother, neither a Republican nor particularly versed in or even concerned about the matters of war politics, refused to speak to me for a week. When I stepped out of my bedroom, she glared at me, walked away, and refused to respond to anything I said. She avoided me in the house, and one evening I ended up having to write her a note saying that I needed money for my school lunch. When I woke up, I found a $5.00 bill wrapped inside of the note—my mother nowhere to be found.

"That's fucked up," Sam, the therapist, says.

"I agree," I say.

I switch jobs. Sam becomes a licensed therapist. He is trained in cognitive behavioral therapy, and he integrates mindfulness exercises into his sessions. He counsels college students with anxiety, depression, and a bevy of other diagnoses. When I ask him what he tells his students, he says he coaches them on how to reorient their thoughts, how to see their worlds from a different perspective. It's in the recognition of the reactions we have, of our gut-level responses, the thoughts themselves—that his patients learn to take control or, in some key situations, to understand the futility of trying to maintain control. I like to think that he teaches them a message that is the opposite of the Christian dogma with which I was raised, though I'm sure he would disagree with this. I picture him saying to his patients, "No god is going to fix your problems. So what are you going to do?"

I have grown tired of unquestioning loyalty, and, in our marriage, this is the promise we keep. We talk. We discuss. We analyze. "If you ever grow tired of . . ." I say in a dozen different combinations.

They were always so mixed up, I say to him. Either that, or they were lazy. No one ever showed them how to make a family. He put food on the table. She stood by his side. I tell him, sometimes I don't think love meant the same thing back then. I say, we can never be like them.

For four years, I keep her at bay. There's silence at first, and then she calls me and leaves me sad voice messages.

I was twenty years old when he picked me up off his driveway. I collapsed in the cold, Maine night, and he could have set me loose. He could have said, this is all too much—I need to be a kid still. He could have said, I need to feel my way into adulthood. I need to live untethered and unbothered and free. He could have sent me back to Providence, said "Good luck," and let me find my own way. He picked me up, and he said, "It's going to be okay. I'm here."

I work the corporate job, and then I take another job, and Sam graduates, and when my little book of short stories is ready, he says "Go!" and he sets me into the world to be an artist. People are always shocked when we say we've been together so long. They raise their eyebrows, as if we couldn't possibly love each other, as if we couldn't possibly, in this day and age, condone staying together with your college sweetheart.

"You either change together or you don't," I say.

Sam says, "Partnership. The key is partnership."

My mother broke the silence twice during those four years. On both occasions, I was ambushed on trips back to West Virginia. She had found out through the small-town rumor mill that I was coming in, and each time she was waiting for me in her car.

The first time was a year after my marriage, in 2013, outside of my ten-year high school reunion. It was summer, and I was in town alone, without Sam. I was nervous about how the redneck men would react if Sam came (still holding onto those fears, those phobias). I had been invited first to have drinks with some old classmates at one of their childhood homes. We sat and drank beer and wine on the porch of this friend's house and caught up about our lives—jobs, spouses, challenges, kids. I didn't mention her to most of them. A few close friends, like Sara, one of my oldest friends whom I'd met in the fourth grade, knew about everything. But in general, I tried not to bring my mother up anymore. My life was Sam, was New York, was writing—all of these wonderful things that had nothing to do with her or our lack of a relationship. I had, in other words, moved on.

She hadn't.

The high-school friends and I walked across town toward the bar where we'd have our reunion. We were just outside when Sara pointed her out. She said something like, "Jon—uh-oh—your mom," and there she was, sitting in her Dodge Stratus, the same car she'd had since before I graduated high school ten years ago. It was old when she bought it. Now it was rusted and looked like it belonged in a junkyard.

I wanted to die. This was supposed to be my chance to strut in front of those redneck boys who'd once made fun of me. I could say, look at me, I live in New York, I married a man, I write stories and eat fun foods and I've traveled around the world. I suppose it was karma for thinking like that. Schadenfreude is never so fun when your own unfinished business is waiting for you in the driver's seat of a rusted-out Dodge Stratus.

I got in the car and I said, "You have five minutes. I'm not doing this. We're not doing this."

The more she aged, the more I thought she looked like one of those antique porcelain dolls: delicate, yellowed, broken in places.

She said, "Please, Jon, talk to me."

I'd been ambushed, and I was genuinely scared. I'd spent so much of my time building up ways to keep her out, to keep myself sane. I relied on my gut then, and I said to her, "You have ten minutes and then I'm leaving. What do you want to say?"

She said, "How are you doing?"

"I am fine." It was not a lie, though in that moment, I felt myself on the edge of reversion—the alarms in my gut went off, sounded a warning that this old way of being could reemerge in the blink of an eye.

She started to ask a question or two. "Where do you work? Do you still live in Brooklyn?"

"Sam is fine. We both have jobs. Life is fine."

I had to keep it short. I had to guard the self that I'd finally found, that I'd worked so hard to keep stable. There was no time to think of this sadness—that a mother would know so little about the life of her son.

Her eyes were wet. She grabbed my hand. Her hand shook.

"We can't do this," I said.

"Please, I miss you," she said. "I love you."

I said, "I love you too, but you need to leave me alone."

"Will you ever—"

I interrupted her. I said, "I don't know. I have to go."

I pulled my hand away, and I exited her car. I was on the verge of hyperventilating.

In the bar, Sara asked, "What did she want?"

I told her, "She wants to pretend like nothing ever happened."

It was a little more than a year later, the fall of 2014, that I came to town for Sara's wedding. In my memory, my mother was waiting there, too, in the parking lot outside of the railroad baron's mansion where Sara wed her husband, but the more I think of it, the more I know that wouldn't be right.

Would she have left me a hundred voicemails? Would she have pushed my sisters to broker the meeting? Sam says that my memory is better than his—and so, as always, I stitch together the details the best I can.

She *was* in her car—that same silver Stratus—at the edge of the city park, the place of so many of our failed meetings. I was not yet in my wedding suit, so it would have been planned, a courtesy. She had called me. We set up a neutral meeting point. I told her that I didn't want to meet at the old house. I told Sam I needed to be somewhere I felt safe, a place from which I could exit quickly. Sam was with me, and we saw her sitting there, eager, in her driver's seat, as we pulled our rental car not far from hers.

We walked to a picnic table, and she got out of her car. She stumbled through the grass. Her walking was worse than I'd ever seen it. For the past decade she had walked in fits and starts—it was the pain, she said, and the doctors would one day confirm that the artery there, where she clutched her leg in agony, was nearly one hundred percent blocked from years of smoking. It took her five minutes to cross the fifty feet of grass to reach us.

She was already crying. She opened her arms. It was the kind of pitiful you hope you'll never have to witness—like watching your spouse descend into dementia or your child die of a rare bone cancer. You are sturdy and this other body that was once so important to you is becoming a bag of bones.

She said, "Will you hug me?"

I walked over to her, stiff as a tetanus patient, and put my arms around her.

"Mother," I said. I gave her a tepid pat on the back.

And then she stumbled over to Sam, and put him into the same awkward embrace. She left both of our shoulders wet.

We sat down opposite each other—Sam and I on one side, one end, and she on the other, across the diagonal.

She lit a cigarette.

"Will you forgive me?" she said. "I cry every night."

This was not news to me. She said the same each time we'd reconciled. I believed her, that she was sorry. I believed that she loved me. I believed that she sat alone in the kitchen, in her bedroom, with the lights turned low, that she stubbed out cigarette after cigarette thinking about where it all went wrong. I knew that she hurt.

There's a voice that certain people use. It sounds like a gentle hand pulling the blanket up to your neck. It sounds like a lullaby. It's a dangerous voice, because it's real and honest, in its way. It sounds like a childhood memory, and it can transport you from the present to the womb. I have learned not to trust this voice.

Sam looked to me for clues. He said to her, "What you did to us was awful."

I said, "I forgive you, but we can't have a relationship."

She grew angry. Her head shook from side to side. She begged and pleaded and cried and sucked on her cigarette.

I remembered everything she had ever told me, sitting in that park. The park bench was like a record player, and she was the record. My father had never treated her right. Her mother never loved her. The man who had touched her when she was just a little girl. She too suffered. She too hurt. She hurt so, so much.

I remembered every truth, every pain, every story.

I said, "I won't ever stop loving you, but we can't do this. You've hurt me too many times."

We stared at each other until it hurt too much. I was looking across the park, thinking about how she told me her mother used to comb the grounds and collect all the black walnuts, the ones with that peculiar citrus smell. Her mother would leave them in a dark place to dry out—to go from green to black. It would take months, but then they'd be ready to crack and eat.

I said good-bye.

She said, "When will I see you again?"

I told her I didn't know, and Sam put one hand on my shoulder blade and steadied me as we walked to the car. I closed the door and put my seat belt on. He started the engine.

"Drive, please. We have to go," I said.

I couldn't look back.

I squeezed Sam's arm and he took me somewhere, elsewhere—I don't remember—but I know that she was gone, out of the mirror, and that I couldn't see her.

In four years without her, I learned how to be a partner in marriage. Despite what I had been taught, despite the tendencies that had been instilled in me, Sam and I learned to fight less, listen more, and lift each other up. I took some time off to finish and publish my first book, and I began to think of myself not as damaged goods, not as someone with family problems, but as someone who chased his dreams, as someone who fought for success.

In four years without her, I took care of my health and my teeth and my mental health, and I learned how easy it is to go to sleep at night when you remove these stressors from your life.

In four years without her, my imagination returned—and I was thinking less and less about the past and more and more about the possibilities of the future.

I loved Sam more each day. I loved myself more each day.

I would surprise myself; there were days, sometimes even weeks, when I found myself so entirely present, so entirely committed to the world in which I lived that I would stop and realize that I hadn't given her a single thought. Entire weeks would go by, and I would concern myself only with what we were having for dinner, what show we would see on Broadway, what story I might edit, what desert we might traverse on vacation.

This did not mean I loved her any less.

She was becoming more dead to me with each passing day, and each day that she died a little in my mind, I seemed to sprout a new branch, a new leaf. It had been so long since I had known what this kind of growth felt like, what it was like to grow physically and emotionally unencumbered.

She called me every month or so. She left voice messages on my phone. She said the devil had been inside her. She said she hurt so much.

I listened to the messages, and then I'd forget them. I'd forget her.

I was so very much alive.

17

My father was dying. It was a long, slow death that had begun even before my mother and I stopped speaking. But after my wedding, my father descended toward the end. I did not call him, and he did not call me. I relied on my sisters, who kept me updated in fits and starts.

First, he dropped a brick on his toe, and the toe didn't heal quite right. Then, he fainted in a ditch at the construction site. Then, when the doctors said his body was giving out—that his body would give out if he didn't make changes—he quit working. He had no health insurance. He had no retirement. His longtime boss did not pay his hospital bills. When the troubles began, he was in his sixties, just shy of receiving Social Security and Medicare. My parents had never had much money, but after my father's health issues, they became very poor for a time, making do with whatever money my mother could scrounge together from cleaning jobs.

My father once had biceps like barrels. He'd been a paratrooper in the army, and a bricklayer for some forty years. His body failed like an aging machine. First it was the toe—diabetes, they said. Then it was his kidneys—years of poor eating. He was nearing end-stage renal failure. He could go on dialysis and prolong his life. My sisters said he refused. He'd rather die free than die tethered to a machine.

I've learned that when it comes to predictions about death, nothing happens as expected. He lingered with his poor kidneys, with his diabetes. He became a shell of himself, I was told. He sat in a faded recliner in the living room. He might work up the energy to drive around town. He didn't have the strength to cheat or gamble. He lost pound after pound and had hollow cheeks.

My mother sat in the house and watched over him. This, she believed, was God's final test. She had stood by his side all those years, and then, at the end, God needed her to take care of him, to shepherd him to the other side.

He was grateful. He said he loved her, that he'd been an awful husband and an awful father. He said that he was blessed to have her in his life, that she'd taken care of their children.

In his final years on earth, my father became a semblance of the husband my mom always wanted. All it took was organ failure.

In February 2016, my sisters told me that he was having open-heart surgery—now there were blockages, things were looking dangerous. He'd lost his hearing, his blood flow, his kidney function. There was no guarantee he'd even survive the surgery.

I debated with Sam for days. Would I care if I never saw him before he died? Would I regret not saying good-bye? My sisters insisted I should see him. I had no relationship with him. During my last conversation with him, more than four years prior to this hospitalization, he'd threatened to come to my wedding and shoot Sam and me with a shotgun. And yet I still called him my father.

I struggled with ambivalence. I could admit to myself that I wouldn't blame myself if I didn't go. We'd had almost no relationship since before I'd even graduated high school. What happened to him mattered more in theory than it did in reality. If he died, I'd have no father, but I'd hardly had one during my thirty years of existence. The reactions I was having weren't devoid of emotion—I cried like anyone, this near-instinctual attachment to a person who didn't deserve my love or thoughts or energy. I never knew if I cried over him or over the idea that things could have been so different, that his loss marked the end of our potential relationship, even if the potential had largely remained theoretical.

To go down there would also mean to see her. She'd be at his side, and I had no interest in rekindling our relationship. His lack of fathering had left holes, but her way of mothering me—the meanness, the back and forth—left open wounds that festered.

Sam remained levelheaded. He said that any decision I made would be understandable. He would go with me or he would stay.

In the end, I think I decided to go out of another type of instinct. It was a desire for justice. I wanted to look him in the eye and let him know that I lived, that I prospered, in spite of him. I wanted him to see me as the man I'd become, and a part of me, though it sounds so cruel, wanted him to own this guilt and stew on it during his last days. He'd never had any accountability in his life. I thought, let him simmer with this truth.

I rented a car, left New York, and drove solo—my choice—to Ruby Memorial Hospital in Morgantown, West Virginia, on February 11, 2016. It was a seven-hour drive across New Jersey, Pennsylvania, Maryland, and then West Virginia. Ruby's one of the state's best hospitals—a sprawling complex of towers and bridges and parking lots. He'd been sent there because our local hospital was too small and ill-equipped to handle such delicate cases.

My sisters were there in the lobby, and we greeted each other. I hadn't seen them in years. It was a somber greeting. They looked tired and worried. It was late, and the hospital only allowed a couple of family members in the room at a time, so they told me to go in, that they'd been there all day, that he'd be happy to see me.

I went in the elevator and walked down the long halls toward his room.

I saw her first, sitting in a chair next to his bed, and then him, his sunken-in cheeks and the oxygen tube. They were skeleton versions of the parents I'd known.

Each time I saw her, I thought it impossible that her cheekbones could protrude further, that her skin could look more sallow. She was not just getting old—she was aged, tired, worn, deflated—I couldn't find enough adjectives.

And yet when she saw me, the child inside her came to life. She poked him, bobbed up and down in her chair, whispered loudly. "Jack, Jack, Jack," she said. "Look who's here."

Her eyes were perpetually wet, it seemed to me, on the verge of or just past tears—it was hard to say. When I arrived, her wet eyes opened wide, glowed like the surface of a river on a hot, sunny day.

He craned his neck, looked at me, turned his head back toward the television. "Hello," he mumbled.

"Jack, Jack," she said. And then I heard just bits of her whisper ". . . your son" and "Jon is here."

The realization sank over him, he lifted himself from his reclined position and sat up.

"Jon," he said. His voice was the last embers of a fire: the cracks, the fight against extinguishment. He had not recognized me. My hair was thinning away. I had a stubbly beard. He had not recognized this version of his boy who had turned some corner on becoming a man.

"Jon is here, Jon is here," she said. Every phrase came out in twos and threes.

I kept my distance—stood three or four feet away, stiff with my back to the door. I felt ready to dart out at the wrong provocation.

My mother jumped up, hobbled her way across the room, and pulled a chair over near the bed. As she neared me, as the air shifted around us, I imagined her touch like a venom of sorts: the kind that would lower my defenses, would let her claim me back, would let her erase from my memory the things she'd said.

"I won't bother you," she said. "Thank you, thank you."

He was not all there—I wasn't sure if he was on sedatives or if this was just who he was now. We spoke in three- and four-word sentences. He didn't seem to have the energy or consciousness for more. I gave him the tiniest facts—Brooklyn, working. I didn't mention my writing. The last time we'd spoken, his body and mind had been whole. He said he'd come to my wedding with a shotgun. And yet here I was, alive, while he was on the edge of death, here in this room that smelled like diapers.

He grabbed my hand and pulled me close. "Good luck with your book," he rattled out. The words bit at me. He fell back into his bed and went to sleep.

I had only come down for a couple of days. I lied and told them I could only stay the night. I wasn't sure I had the strength to deal with another day of this. I would spend another night with a friend who lived nearby. I'd leave before he regained consciousness after the surgery.

Good luck with your book.

It was the last thing he said to me.

Before I left the hospital, my mother followed me into the hall. She fell into me. I had no choice in the matter. She hugged me, and cried.

"Thank you, thank you, thank you," she said. Her body quaked so much that a passerby might have thought she was on drugs.

"This means so much," she said. "Really, it means so much."

She wouldn't let me go. She clung to my shirt, kept her crying eyes pressed into my shoulder.

"I won't bother you," she said again.

It was pitiful. My sisters had gone away for the night. I was alone with her in the hallway. We were surrounded by the broken, the dying.

"Please forgive me," she said.

I had promised myself that I wouldn't let this moment happen. I promised myself that I wouldn't let her back in—not now, just when the old scars had started to fade.

"Please, please, please," she said. And when she spoke like that, in those desperate threes, I couldn't not think back to how over the years, he'd left her with nothing but a gender, how he'd stripped her down to wife, to *woman, woman, woman,* and soon, his widow.

I made her no promises, but I couldn't see her suffer.

"I love you," I said.

It was the only thing that I could ever say to her that was true.

I left the hospital. I wasn't convinced I'd ever see her or him again. I hoped she'd take my small words and hold onto them, that they'd be enough to get her through.

My short story collection came out in April of that year. It was my first book, and I planned a ramshackle tour with some twenty stops across the East and West Coasts. The book was coming out from a university press, and it wasn't likely to get much attention unless I hustled, so that's what I did. I made a stop in basically any city where I knew a handful of people who'd show up to a reading.

It was the best and worst time of my life. It seemed he was dying every day, and I felt haunted by what he'd said—"Good luck with your book," like he knew anything about my life, like he cared, like he regretted his choices. To admit that he was human—to start seeing any of them as human—meant dropping my armor, making myself vulnerable, and a first-book tour was not supposed to be that time.

The book contained stories set in a fictional West Virginia town, not unlike the one I'd grown up in. There were stories about gay people and straight people, many of whom grappled with the choice to stay or go. There were details from my real life that I'd used to craft this world, but no one seemed to understand how fiction worked. At all the readings, the audience wanted to know what it was like growing up there, gay, in that little dying town—

"It's fiction—" I'd started at first, but then I soon relented.

My father was dying, my mother and I still weren't speaking, and I ended up on a twenty-town tour talking about the struggles of growing up gay in Appalachia.

I'd scheduled a handful of stops in West Virginia, including one in my hometown. I was scared, because I thought that an increasingly conservative West Virginia couldn't handle someone like me coming through and reading passages from a book that was at times loving and critical, that contained several openly and unapologetically gay story lines. It was 2016, and Trump was beginning his ascent. The country had gone mad; we were beginning once again to reveal our violent side. I told my friends that I was so scared, so nervous, that I feared people heckling me or walking out—or worse, like my father had once threatened, opening fire.

My father had been in and out of hospitals for the previous two months, after I'd seen him just before his open heart surgery. He had survived the surgery, but it hadn't been without complications. A part of his heart was infected. He was sent to a VA hospital in Pennsylvania. He was not doing well.

He was like a dog, in his final weeks, waiting for me to return. The day I arrived in my hometown for my reading, the hospital sent him home to spend his last days in hospice. My mother had set up a hospital bed in the room where I had once slept, where I'd listened to them fight for so many years, where I'd for some time cried myself to sleep begging God not to make me gay.

My sisters told me the news, and then my mother called me and I picked up. She did not want to talk about my father. She instead begged me for permission to attend my reading. I consented.

I organized my reading at the local community theatre, the Old Brick Playhouse, where I'd once fumbled as the Tin Man in search of a heart. It was the same community theatre that she'd forced me to quit because she thought the staff were "funny," which meant that she thought they were gay, which meant, I now know, that she thought they were turning me gay.

It was not a particularly large crowd. Maybe forty people showed up in a theatre designed for three or four times that. A part of me thought I would have some huge homecoming, that I'd have my "local boy makes good" moment. I tried to count any number of people as a win, particularly that since I'd arrived in West Virginia, I'd begun to feel like a sort of gay evangelical, traveling and spreading the good word through my quiet, lyrical musings. I was a gay evangelical or a gay debutante. I had never had some official coming-out with the people of my hometown.

Before I went on stage, I saw her there in the audience. I walked up to her. I gave her a reluctant hug. I said, "Mother," in a voice I'd calculated to reveal no vulnerability. I said, "I'm glad you're here."

I wavered about what I was going to read until the last moment. I decided to read the title story from my collection: "The Rope Swing." The story takes place on a secluded riverfront. It's about two boys who are falling in young love with each other. One is beginning to break free, and the other is too afraid to admit the truth. In the story, they'd met at the community theatre, and they whispered backstage about hopes, dreams, and oppressive mothers.

It was the right choice, to read that story. When I looked around I saw this one older woman in the audience. I recognized her, but I didn't know her name. She became my focus. She kept nodding her head, up and down, knowingly. She thanked me after, told me that my words were important.

In the end, I decided I would never again be the scared boy from my story.

There were celebrations, of course, with friends. There were drinks afterward and there were toasts and old stories. I had a week-long break after the hometown reading, with only a few more stops— Kentucky, Virginia, and then DC—before I drove back to New York. But all my hope for rest, for basking in the joy of launching a book, disappeared the next day.

I went to my house to see my father. We were all there—my mother, my two sisters, my skeletal father sleeping in my old bedroom. The hospice nurse arrived, and she gave us the straightforward lecture that she gave to all her patients. This is how you use the dispenser to suck up the morphine. This is how you put it in his mouth.

"I *will* measure the liquid each day," she said. "No offense."

The comment couldn't have been any less jarring, though we all understood that there was an opioid epidemic ravaging the state.

The nurse explained that the more we used the morphine, the more his body would slow down, the closer he would come to death. I don't think she could officially say that we were assisting him toward the end, that we were speeding up what could be an overly slow, messy process. But I thought I heard her gist. If we were tired, if he was driving us mad with his wailing, with his nightmares, we could drip the morphine into his mouth, maybe just a little more than we had before, and we'd bring him closer to the moment when his body would just stop.

I volunteered to sit with him and with her. I had not been in close contact with anyone in my family for so long, but there I was, at the end of his life, stuck in my town for a week, seemingly by accident. No matter what my relationship had been with them, I couldn't see a way out of this.

My sisters and I took turns. One of us would sprawl across the couch and nap while my mother would take the bed. We were to watch him, keep him in our line of sight, my old bedroom door kept open. He was on oxygen, and he was rarely conscious, and even then, he could barely get more than a word out. It was unclear whom or what he recognized.

He'd toss in his sleep, and he'd yank the oxygen tube from his nose, and we'd take turns putting it back on his face, only for him to bat it away again. My mother looked desiccated, as she lamented that she didn't know what to do, not with the oxygen tube, not with his moaning, not with her unbrushed hair. She'd throw her hands up and bury her head in the corner of the couch, and then one of us would grab the morphine nervously and drip it into his mouth. I eventually took the lead on the morphine.

I could not change his diapers. That was my limit. I'm not sure I even verbalized this choice, but my sisters and my mother let me use my maleness to skirt by. Men don't change diapers, men don't wipe up the shit of their babies, whether childlike or geriatric. I was a kid again, trying to help my mom wash dishes, and there was my father, chastising me for my effort—"Men don't do the dishes," he'd said. "Get away from the sink."

I didn't want to change his diapers precisely because he had never changed mine. My dying father had done nothing to earn this kindness. I could shove morphine into his mouth. I could help him leave this world, just as he had once helped me enter it, but that was as far as I could assist.

During his week of hospice, old friends came out of the wood-work to see him one last time. There were neighbors and friends and old veterans and old construction workers. Everyone loved him, it seemed. Over and over we heard stories of his high jinks running around the bars, running around the town. I introduced myself over and over. Half of the visitors didn't know he'd had a son.

It was the same story I'd heard my whole life. Everyone loved Jack. He'd kept his word, lent money freely, told the best jokes. He'd taken care of everyone, it seemed, save his own kin.

The moaning and the tossing and turning increased day by day. He was not lucid. In his sleep we heard him talking.

"What is he saying?" one of my sisters asked.

"He was chasing a squirrel," someone in the room said.

This is my penultimate memory of his life. My father, in his last days, dreamt of squirrel hunting.

I gave him the morphine. I didn't add any extra. I gave him what the nurse said was allowed. There was no point in holding back. There was no point in prolonging the inevitable. I was alone in the room with him, and I had nothing left to say. I whispered in his ear, "You can die now."

He died the next day.

I cannot remember if I was there when he took his last breath.

The undertakers arrived to carry out his body. My family lined up in the house to watch them, our bodies pressed against the walls, as the white-shirted men carried him to the hearse.

After my father's death, Sam rushed down from New York to be at my side.

My mother said, "I now know God put Sam on this earth as your guardian angel," and "We're a family," and something about the devil inside her and "Never again."

He died on Monday, May 2, 2016, and I had a reading sched-uled at a bookstore in Washington, DC, the following day. My family decided not to hold a funeral. There were money issues, I think, but I didn't feel the need to take part in these discussions. I'd been gone for too long. They would cremate his body and mail me a portion of the ashes. That would suit me just fine, I said.

I decided I'd spent too much of my life giving up opportunities, and I'd decided that giving him my attention during the week in hospice had been enough. I wasn't callous. I ached, in fact, once again over the notion of what could have been and what now would never be. So I said good-bye to my family, and I told my mother we would speak soon, and Sam drove me to Washington.

In the car, I asked him what I should do—about her—and he said, she's changed a lot, but who's to say—and there was no way *to say*. He'd seen it all. I told him that I'd seen something in her—something that suggested she too was descending toward an end—and I said, we'll do it my way.

I kept thinking of the adage that one should keep your enemies close, but I wasn't sure if she was my enemy. I told Sam, I'll let her in, but I'll keep her at a distance. I had tried and tried and tried. It was best to maintain control, I said, to dictate the terms.

After he died, it wasn't long before she suffered a stroke. I drove to West Virginia to be by her side in the hospital. The doctors scanned her brain and said there had been more, at least three or four ministrokes that had gone undetected. She survived, but the strokes took bits of her, little by little, the parts so small that you couldn't see them unless you'd known her for a lifetime.

I called her once a month until the very end. I think by then she understood that was as good as we'd ever get. When I went back to West Virginia, maybe once a year, I'd stay in hotels or at friends' homes. I'd take her out to a bench in the city park for lunch, and we'd eat subs and drink diet soda and smoke cigarettes. She'd apologize for the devil that had been inside her. She'd tell me, once again, about Neale's Drug Store, about missed opportunities, of all the times she'd chased my father.

18

My mother told me stories about her father. She didn't know his name, but she swore she had met him once or twice.

"I was a little girl," she would say, "and there was this man in a trench coat out on the railroad tracks in South Elkins. He'd walk the train tracks and throw pennies on the rail."

She'd follow him down the tracks, grabbing the pennies as she went. The way she described it was like a fairy tale. He would appear and throw his coins, and she'd smile and laugh and skip right after him. She had no fear. This was not a threatening man.

And I would ask, "How did you know it was him?"

"It was a feeling," she'd say. "A person just knows."

She spoke of her childhood so infrequently that the man on the track seemed more real to me than her other family members. I'd hardly spent any time with my grandmother or her aunts and uncles—though they had confirmed names, they were so absent from my life that I could never remember them. The man on the tracks, then, became my true lineage. I could almost draw his face.

She would see him again years later, this time at the front door. She was living in our house, married. My oldest sister was a baby, asleep in her crib—not old enough to remember. A man knocked, and though my mother was home alone, she answered. He was in a trench coat—always the mysterious trench coat—with a suit and tie underneath. He was an older man. The right age. Handsome.

He asked if Jack was home.

She hesitated. She shouldn't be telling strangers at the door that she was home alone. But she didn't hesitate long, because she was not scared. This man meant her no harm.

No, she said, but he'd be home later.

And the man—her apparition of a father—paused, took her in, took a peek inside.

Could she give his name? Could she tell Jack who was calling? The man did not identify himself. He said he'd come back later. He left. She never saw him again.

She said, "He was coming to check up on my husband. He wanted to see who married his daughter."

And she was always so matter of fact when I asked her to repeat the story.

"I truly believe it was him," she'd say.

My mother spent seventy-two years dreaming about her father. Absence has a way of spreading. The hole my grandfather left in my mother's life, the hole that kept her searching, that at times made her feel empty, abandoned, and even hopeful—as she dreamed that he might return, might reveal himself, might apologize, might begin to fill the missing things she could not name—that hole has at times worked itself into my own life.

For so long I said that one-quarter of my heritage was missing. This can be taken superficially. I don't think that I truly cared so much about the supposed ethnicity of my grandfather, about his point of origin. I would be no different if he were Irish, German, or Native American, all of which had been proposed by my mother. But we live in a world that assigns value to this knowing. We live in a world that values clear and decipherable lineages, that values the ability to draw a straight line and draw sometimes spurious conclusions about who we are, why we do the things we do. Look at her hotheadedness! Look at those noble cheekbones!

For a long time, I resisted buying into this way of thinking. I was gay, my mother had disowned me—why should I care about my blood relations, about the people who had treated me so callously? But with time, with so much unfinished business, as my relationship with my mother seemed locked in a stalemate, I suppose that I, like others, found myself looking for explanations. I had mined every bit of her life that I knew. I thought that, just maybe, some detail in this man's biography might explain it—explain why my mother would stay with my father, why she had, like her own father, abandoned her child, why we could never be whole.

But how could I find him? My mother would sit and dream up stories, and sometimes those stories had a way of becoming her beliefs, and then I would sit and try to decipher the reality from the fiction. The man on the railroad tracks was a ghost, yet also made of flesh and blood. The man who had come to our door, too, seemed to me equal parts apparition and solid. I don't know what I thought—who I thought he would be. I supposed he was lurking somewhere in our small town, and, like my mother, I supposed he knew about her, about us. I gathered that I probably wouldn't like the man—someone who would leave my grandmother in the lurch, someone who would never reveal himself. I had begun to resent him, if for no other reason than the conversational awkwardness he caused. It seemed the whole world had been programmed to ask, "Who are you?" and "Where do you come from?"

"I guess I'm Irish."

"No, my grandmother never told her."

"I have not asked my grandmother."

"I do not speak to my mother."

"There is no need to be sorry."

In the end, I too wanted more than anything to know the identity of this man, because I was beginning to see that he was responsible for some part of our cycle. I don't know if I had the courage to call it abuse. But the cycle that he had started or had participated in—the rash love, the abandoning, the leaving in the lurch—was still going strong. In the end, I believed that the story of this unknown man's life and purpose was somehow destined to explain the things that I did not understand about my own, might even contain the key to finally end the circles of pain that seemed to consume and connect us.

It would be a decidedly modern advancement that would lead me to him. I had been bombarded by the ads for years. People finding out about countries of origin. People finding the faces of three-hundred-year-old ancestors. People understanding their absurd love of bagpipes. I had hesitated, like many others, for fear of what the companies would do with my DNA. But the missingness, the desire to know, prevailed.

I purchased the kit late in 2018. I held onto it for nearly a year. I don't know why it took me so long. I might have been lazy or busy, but I think a part of me was afraid of what I might find. I spit in the cup in the summer of 2019, and the results came back in September. The first thing I noticed was that I was supposedly much more English than Irish—53 percent to 23 percent—which, given my surname and my blue eyes, was the reverse of what I'd expected.

There was nothing else terribly interesting about my background. And for a while, I was disappointed. I guess I'd built up some kind of hope that there would be something more unexpected, something that the mirror couldn't tell me. I guess I'd been hoping for some Italian or Russian or who knows what kind of ancestor—something far enough from my daily existence to let my imagination run wild, that would make the man on the railroad tracks come to life as more than just a sad story. But I was English and Irish, and for those first few hours after receiving my test, nothing about my life changed. I was, rationally, who I had always been.

The shock would come when I began to comb through the familial matches—the people who had also uploaded tests and shared parts of my DNA. There were relatives and names that I recognized. There were hundreds of extremely distant matches who were sixth or seventh cousins from some shared great-great-great-grandparent. It was hard to be excited for these folks who seemed little more than names in a phone book. But there were a few names that made no sense. Katherine ——, Sally ——, extremely close matches, first or second cousins (I've altered their names for privacy). I had never heard of these people. I clicked on them, and I explored their family trees to find the mutual aunt or uncle. But there was nothing. And then the more I combed through the results, the more I found other DNA matches that I shared with no other members of my extended family, the more I realized I had stumbled onto something—a man's name—something potentially huge.

I wrote this message to Katherine:

Hi Katherine,

I hope this note finds you well. This is going to be somewhat of an odd letter. I'm trying to find the best way to put this all down here. My name is Jonathan Corcoran. I live in Brooklyn, NY now, but I'm originally from a small town in West Virginia called Elkins. I just received my AncestryDNA results, and I noticed that we had a very close cousin match. I took a look at your family tree on here, and I think—I'm not 100% sure, but I'm almost certain—that you've just helped me solve a family mystery. I hope this doesn't sound rude. I believe that your grandfather, John Clarence Bennett, is also my grandfather.

I'm going to try to explain this all here. It's a somewhat complicated story, so forgive me if this sounds strange or confusing. My mother, Patty Corcoran, grew up never knowing who her father was (and I grew up never knowing who my grandfather was). She was born in 1946, the oldest child of several siblings, but she didn't share the same father as any of her siblings. Her mother, born June Ware, had had some sort of affair or one night stand or something that was considered scandalous back in the forties, and I believe it was with John Clarence Bennett (from your tree). My grandmother was so ashamed of getting pregnant outside of marriage that she refused to tell my mother the name of her father. My grandmother June married shortly after my mother was born, had all of my uncles and aunts with this new HUSBAND, and took the name of my mother's father to her grave. My grandmother died a few years ago. I honestly know very little information about the circumstances surrounding my mother's birth. My grandmother was very private and very ashamed of this situation.

My mom had friends and neighbors who had insinuated that her father was a "Bennett" man, and she'd even heard once that his name was "John Bennett," but she'd never found him or found any way to prove this. Again, her own mother refused to talk about it. My mother had somewhat of a troubled childhood as a sort of illegitimate stepchild, and she never much got along with my grandmother.

When I saw your tree—and our surprising genetic match—I realized that this man, John Clarence Bennett, is most likely my mother's father. He grew up and spent time in the same rural parts of West Virginia that my grandmother would have spent time in during the same times. I grew up hearing stories from my mother of all the people who had told her that her father was a "Bennett" man, and it seems to all add up. And now there is a genetic component to this. I'm not sure I could explain this any other way.

If this is true, this means that your father would have been my mother's half brother, my mother your aunt. It also means that I would be your first cousin. I have two sisters who are older than me (I'm 34). Their names are Jackie (Corcoran) Simmons and Teresa Corcoran.

I hope this doesn't sound too strange. I guess I'm writing to see if you have ever heard anything like this from your own family members, to see if there were ever any rumors. If this is all true, it would be very meaningful to me and my sisters, and especially to my mother, to learn anything about this side of our family—particularly about John Clarence, and also about your father, who would have been my uncle, my mother's half brother.

I always hear of these strange stories coming from Ancestry, so I'm not exactly sure what happens next. I appreciate your reading this, and I know it probably sounds very strange.

That said, I would love to hear more from you. I'd be more than happy to chat on the phone down the road if this isn't too much.

Thanks again,
Jonathan Corcoran

Katherine wrote me back and told me that she had forwarded the message onto her cousin, Sally. It wasn't long until Sally reached out.

Sally was the family expert. She said she'd been researching this man and his descendants for more than two decades. The parallels between our mothers and grandmothers' stories were nearly identical. Her grandmother had also taken her secret, this man's name, to the grave. Her mother had also heard whispers of a "Bennett." Her family had grown up in West Virginia, in Webster Springs, the same place where John Clarence Bennett, or JCB as she called him, had lived before joining the navy in World War II.

Unbelievably, Sally turned out to be an actual genealogist. I sent her my DNA results, and she confirmed the match—she explained the science, which checked out, though that didn't much matter to me at the time. I had found this man. I had found the missing link. I had found my grandfather. I found my mother's father. Sally even sent me pictures.

What I found out about him broke my heart.

He had left a string of children across the Eastern seaboard, at least seven. He had married four times, one woman twice. Many of his children shared the same story. Sally said:

> In my business, I prefer to work with Adoptees and Long Lost Family members, I have seen A LOT of circumstances just like JCB. When I started searching, I had hoped that JCB would be different than my expectations. From what I've gathered from my research, he wasn't. I believe that he couldn't commit to one woman, decided to have his fun at the cost of several women and their children and I absolutely believe there are more ——'s, ——'s, and Patty's out there that belong to JCB. There is a LARGE gap of time between your Mom's birth and his marriage in 1959.

Sally said:

"The damage that illegitimacy does to a child in the 30's and 40's is very damaging to their character, personality, and confidence."

And: "Please let your Mom know that I completely understand the deep river of hurt, confusion, and quest for truth. She is not alone."

I received these confirmations from Sally, and I shared the photographs and the stories—unfiltered—with my mother.

If she was disappointed, she did not say. What she said was thank you. She said to know that she was glad, after all these years, to know his name, to see his face.

In just a few months after learning his name, my sisters would call to inform me that my mother had been hospitalized with dementia. A few weeks after that, as Covid-19 began to rear its head in America, Sam and I could see the inevitable coming. We raced down to West Virginia to see her one last time, just days before New York City would go into lockdown.

I had given her his name. On that trip I gave her a final hug and told her that I loved her.

She was in the early stages of dementia, but the signs were there. She was there, and she wasn't.

Sam and I had been trying to buy an apartment, before Covid shut everything down. She held out her hand and a $20.00 bill. She received Social Security and had no money left to her name. She said, "For your down payment."

I will never forget how, when we said good-bye, her eyes seemed incapable of focusing, how she looked through me. In that moment, I thought she looked so much like the photos of her father.

19

The date approaches. I've been telling friends that we're taking a trip down to see my family, and the reaction is, *Oh, that's nice,* and sometimes, *How are your parents?*

They are dead, I want to say, *and my memories are unsettled.*

But I don't say such things to my friends, who mean no harm. My family has always been a vague thing to most of the people in my life—alive or dead, my family members have always been the ones who caused me pain or the ones from another world, and my friends have struggled to balance the right amount of inquisitiveness with the right amount of respectful distance to soften the subject. *It was a hard year,* I say and jostle them to remember, and then they leaf through the annals of social media and rifle through long-forgotten text messages and emails, somewhere between the sirens and the bodies and the variants and the vaccines, and then and there or maybe an hour later they say, *I am so sorry. It has been such an awful year for you.*

I too forget sometimes.

It's Friday, June 25, and we're at the World Trade Center and then on the PATH train to pick up a rental car in Jersey City because it's cheaper to rent across the Hudson and then on to the seven-hour drive down to West Virginia. And the truth is I still don't know exactly what or who it is that I'm looking for, what to call this book, why I'm sitting at this desk recalling this trip. Am I looking to find the boy in the photograph, his hand gesturing toward the creek? The mother who eludes me still? I don't tell Sam that we are driving four hundred miles at the very least to see a dogwood tree. A kousa dogwood tree—whatever the hell that is—with the ashes of my mother and my father seeping down into the soil, filtering through the roots.

I am going to see my sisters and my friends and all the dogwood trees of my youth and all the other trees that I climbed upon, shaded under, dreamed about. I am driving four hundred miles to see trees and rivers and creeks and mountains and to look upon a dogwood tree that I am pretending to believe contains the essence of my dead mother. I have forgotten how to grieve, and there hasn't been a funeral, and I have convinced myself that the mystery to mourning is in the leaves of a dogwood tree that seemingly won't die.

We drive through New Jersey and we drive through that wretched stretch of Pennsylvania; when I smell the farm smells on I-78 and we see the faded billboard for shearling jackets, exit 19, it's just another summer trip back home and everyone is still alive and Sam is making the same threat he's been making since 2004 about how he wants so badly to pull off the road and buy one of those tan and white sheepskin coats.

I don't tell Sam that every billboard and every memory has me on the verge of tears and that if I were alone in the car driving myself I would be playing Fleetwood Mac's "Silver Springs" and wailing and crying to that plaintive line that Stevie repeats over and over at the end. Instead, I tell him that I am tired and sad and anxious, and I play "Silver Springs" and sing along until I can't sing anymore because I know that the dam is about to break.

When I get to West Virginia I will have the same conversation with at least a half-dozen people. They will say, "It was hard up there in New York, wasn't it?" They always seem to end on that question, and I realize, like a veteran of a war, a cliché that is so overplayed but still feels like the only relevant way to describe how it felt, that I am incapable of verbalizing to strangers what it was like being sick, thinking you are dying, having your mother die while you are sick, being stuck in your head with unfinished memories and unfinished business while the sirens of a hundred ambulances sound outside your window.

Part Three

In the weeks leading up to the trip, on the drive down, upon our arrival, I drip to Sam that I am struggling, that I am hurting, that I have a lifetime of soreness from which I am recovering. Of course he knows this. He always knows all the things about myself before I do. He drives steadily. He goes five miles over the speed limit, never more. He lets me come to what I need to know. He lets me look out the window at the Pennsylvania farms and meditate on faded billboards for sheepskin coats and the curious roundness of the Pennsylvania hills, and he pretends not to see my eyes moisten when "Silver Springs" plays. I do not say what Sam already knows, but I begin to understand that I am driving four hundred miles to see a kousa dogwood tree because I am tired of living with the weight of thirty-five years of my mother's troubles, that when I see that tree, I want to know that she is buried and gone and that it is safe to open the blinds and that the ambulances are not coming to take her or me or anyone else that I love.

We drive and I sing and I remember. Sam and I have this tradition where I make him play "Country Roads" as we cross the border from Virginia into West Virginia. John Denver's version is a little sacrosanct, but I prefer a version recorded by Dolly Parton to Denver's original. And that's what we do: As we cross over on this trip of memory and grief, as we harmonize to the chorus and belt the bridge, as her backup singers fill the space with four-part drama, the song lets me treat this trip like the homecoming I need it to be.

"Country Roads" fades, but the mountains are everywhere. We pass over the high peaks near the ski resorts in Tucker County, and then we drive down the steep grade past Canaan Valley and up and down again through the waves of trees in the Monongahela National Forest, which surrounds my hometown. It's in those mountains and in those trees—spruce, sycamore, poplar, burning maple—that I can remember my father driving me on a Sunday, how often he repeated the same stories and the same lines. There he'd wrecked the truck drunk, had taken out three towering power-line poles. There he'd had a woman under a tree when he was eighteen

211

or sixteen or who knows what teenage number. There, there, and there—his finger, his cigarette, the ripped vinyl seats of the truck.

"Your mother," he'd say, a lit cigarette in his left hand out the driver's side window of his pickup truck, me looking down over a cliff to the hundred-foot drop into the ravine below. "Your mother, she'll never be happy."

He'd drive up the slim forest road, gravel and pockmarked, stirring up dust as we ascended up to the fire tower on Bickle Knob, elevation 4,003 feet. We'd climb the mesh metal steps and look out at the mountains from the uppermost platform over the top of the tree line for what felt like a hundred miles round.

"Your mother," he'd say, and he'd see something out there, in the trees. "She's not quite right."

What was I to say? It was the same stories, the same lines—age five, age eight, age ten—until seemingly all the stories had been recounted, all the lessons imparted, all the elegies spoken to the wind. One day we stopped driving on these trips at all—Sunday drives, cigarette smoke, concrete dust no more.

On this trip I'll take Sam to all those same places where my father's memory lives—to the boulders up at Bear Heaven, to the fish hatchery, to that tall, rickety fire tower on Bickle Knob, and I'll drip, drip, drip to Sam in my awkward way that I'm trying to see it all once again so that I can let it go, so that I can bury these ghosts of my dead parents. Sam will go along. He'll walk quickly or slowly, in silence or in chatter. He'll follow my lead because he knows that I'm hurting. We'll drive up that same cliffside road to Bickle Knob in our rental car with the low suspension, and the gravel will bounce and crack at the underside of the car, and as we climb, the tires of our car will crunch the gravel and stir up dust storms, and I won't be able to find the words then, but the metaphor sticks—I will tread over the jagged roads of my memories, and all the feelings and pain and joy and sorrow stir up like the dust clouds on a winding forest road, and for a while, I'll be covered in the dust of memory, and Sam will grab my hand and the dust will settle and some of it will stick to my skin. *Then wash.*

Sam and I will climb the fire tower at Bickle Knob, and my heart will race because I have developed a fear of heights. I will look out to the north, to the east, to the south, to the west. I will see the trees, the mountains, the town. I will see her and myself everywhere I look.

We arrive in the evening on Friday, June 25, and we're too tired to go visiting my family, so we head straight to my friend Emily's house, where we're staying. Her home is an enormous relic of the postbellum Civil War. In her home are the original gas lamp fixtures on the wall, wooden floors from the turn of the century. Each time we visit, she's remodeled another room. She's been remodeling for a decade with no end in sight. Yet, unfinished, the big hunk of a house still feels like home.

I've been staying with Emily more or less each summer since she bought the house. Even when my mother and I were having one of our good phases, I couldn't bring myself to break the rules I'd created—to keep distance at all cost, that to sleep in a room next to my mother risked her losing it once again, losing the fragile peace we'd created, ultimately losing her. Our decade and a half of fighting has taught me to always have a space for retreat, a safe space to lay one's head down at night. Emily and her home have been just that.

In fact, Emily and her family have always been my refuge. I've known her since I was nine years old, and we've each gone through our own tough times and hard knocks and big life changes. Just as I find myself finding some kind of womblike comfort in her big, beautiful guest room with the big bright windows and the dozen or so plants, I must have spent half my youth at her childhood home hiding from what awaited me back on Weese Street, back at my own home. Her mom, Helen, was divorced and a highly educated hippie who had grown up in the DC suburbs. She was an English professor at the local college who smoked pot openly, drank white wine in the afternoon, and dabbled with a group of old women who considered themselves witches. Helen kept candles burning, jams playing, goddesses plastered to the walls. Even now, when I go to visit Emily, I feel bereft if I can't stop by and visit her mom to check in, to take in the yellow light reflecting off of her green kitchen walls. When I see Helen, she proffers wine and grapes and a bowl, asks me about writing and books, and remembers the times I showed up crying or nervous at her front door.

"She unplugged Christmas!" Helen cackles when I visit, and I laugh, too, because that was the absurd truth. This is her favorite recollection, that particularly traumatic Christmas when I—all of sixteen years old—showed up at her house and announced that my mother had canceled Christmas. There was always some camp in my pronouncements—I'd thrown open Helen's front door on Christmas Eve, hands in the air, my head shaking in disbelief: "My mother canceled Christmas!" I'd learn to exaggerate in that house, Helen's house of stories, because that was how you made sense of an absurd world, not by hiding the details, but by grabbing them, screaming them, embellishing them over a glass of wine.

The days before my mother had canceled Christmas, we'd all been fighting: I with my sisters, my mother with my father. My mother snapped—viciously, violently, like when she'd broken all the glass when I was kid. She'd been snapping more and more with each passing year; there was hardly anything left to break. She ripped the cord from the wall outlet on Christmas Eve, and the Christmas tree went dark. She screamed and screamed, and then out went the lights outside the house. She announced, "Christmas is over until you learn to love each other!"

I ran to Emily, to Helen's. We drank wine and toasted to my mother, to the end of Christmas, to the pipe dream of dysfunctional families ever learning to love each other.

I am thinking now of what it means to love someone like family. I am thinking of Helen's kitchen table, her eternal glass of wine, her open door. I am thinking of how her home has always had an open door for every troubled child, every lonely street miscreant. When I would visit as a child, there was always a stranger sleeping on her couch.

Early on after my mother disowned me, I was on one of those clandestine trips back to Elkins, the ones I took to hold tight to what was left, to convince myself that my mother couldn't take everything from me. I was visiting Emily and we went to see Helen and Helen found out that my mother had cut me off and she said, "You will stay here."

It was an offer, a fact, a command—all these things. Of course we talked about the details of what had happened, why I thought she'd done what she'd done, but there was no deep discussion about what it meant for me. There was no long, lingering sobbing over how I would survive, how I would exist without a family. Helen said, "You will stay here," and though I never did—I always stayed with her daughter, my dear Emily, I knew that Helen's door remained open, that a bed or a couch could be mine with no notice. In my life I have been a lot of mothers' children, and Helen's certainly.

Helen, Emily, their homes—they were shelter. They provided shelter. They sheltered. To shelter means to protect someone, to provide a roof, both real and figurative, and as I return once again to Elkins, I walk into the door of Emily's home and I think of her mother and that old house, still standing, the door still open, as always, to the kitchen and the wine and the grapes and the marijuana-packed bowl and the witches and the strangers on the sofa. I think of sheltering and mothering and whether these two words mean the same thing.

I realize I have spent so much time seeking shelter from the ones who should have been my protectors and how, even now, I try to keep wine in the fridge, try to keep my front door open, that the memories of the ones who kept me alive and going are in every place I've ever lived, that when people say it is amazing that I am still in touch with old friends from high school, it's so hard to explain what it meant to be taken in, to be protected, to be assured. The Emilys, the Helens, the Gerrys, the Mandys, the Lynnes—all these women who sheltered and held and mothered me as I worked my way back to being whole.

Helen said that her old, clapboard covered place had once been a boardinghouse, and that she'd seen in a vision that there were only good ghosts there.

When we arrive at Emily's, we walk through the front door of her big, old house, and eventually she wanders through her halls and finds us, and she says, "Welcome home."

The next morning, I expect to head straight to Teresa's trailer, but she texts not to come by until the early evening—she needs to clean and she's just had a medical procedure that's making it hard to stay on her feet and she's very much behind. I tell Sam we should go take some walks to kill the time.

We head downtown and grab a coffee. We stand outside the new coffee shop with the vegan sandwiches, and we look north, west, east, south—there are mountains everywhere. Today they feel green, gentle, inviting, protecting. We could go to those mountains this morning—and when I see Sam looking out at them, I can see how their beauty beckons. We could get lost in the forests and the sounds of the canopy blowing in the wind and turn over rocks looking for the elusive Cheat Mountain salamander, but that's not what I have in mind today. Instead, I tell Sam we're going to walk around town—by these three- and four-story buildings built by the railroad barons who were sure that this place would one day be a metropolis. Sam obliges, even though I catch him looking out there, to the green places we could be instead. We walk, and I take him block by block through my memories.

My old friend Sara, who lives in Richmond now, says she has a hard time visiting because of all that has changed. The people, the stores, the other things that she can't quite name. I feel this intensely as I walk with Sam, as I try to conjure a vision of the place I knew, of the place that shaped me. Gone is the bookstore and café, my dad's pawnshop, half the bars (and surely half his women). The health-food store has downsized and moved to a tiny space across the street. The old health-food store now sells hunting equipment, deer blinds.

"My father laid all those bricks," I say, and "My father placed all those marble slabs on the post office."

He laid brick and block for more than forty years. His hands are everywhere.

But then I regress. I become the world's worst tour guide, telling stories only I can understand.

"There's where the G. C. Murphy's stood, where Sara and Emily and I would sneak up the back firewell and dream up stories of murder and mayhem because of the blood on the stairwell. It was just paint, I think, but we *knew* it was blood."

"That's where the hippie lady sold crystals and read charts and let Maya clean the whole house for ten bucks or something, but I don't know where she is—is she still alive?"

"Seneca Mall! Lai Wan Jewelry! Those beads!"

I want so badly for him to see through my eyes that I stop and pause and point and narrate and describe—the black-and-white tile floors, the scent of incense and patchouli, the electric whir of an escalator. I show him where I chipped my front tooth, where I ran down the alley to hide from my father, where my mother lived alone for the only time in her life, above Neale's Drug Store (gone), above the soda fountain (gone), above the makeup counter (gone) where she once dreamed of being a cosmetologist. She said she would look out the window at the people coming and going ("No one walks anymore," she'd said). Even twenty years ago—back when I lived at home—she said the town had become so quiet, that the whole place was dying.

Everything's changed. Everything's gone.

Sam says the town doesn't look so bad. He points to the new coffee shop, the bike shop, the yoga studio, the flower baskets hanging from the bridge. And yes, I see this effort, the ones who stay and try. I cannot tell if he believes what he is saying or if he is just trying to cheer me up. All I can see is decay—the shell of what was, the balance all broken. The hippies are dying out, I say to Sam, replaced by homophobes, racists, Trump voters. They made their own cancer, I think, and year by year they keep pushing out all the good cells, the bright and healthy ones, and what's left is this—a bombed-out relic of a town, this diseased body, all the people driving in circles and waiting for a miracle cure. It's overly simplistic, I suppose, but as I walk through the town I want to grab the good ones, the troubled youth, to push them up and out over the mountains, to share with them the gospel of living free.

I worry that I'm too negative, that I'm only seeing the darkness, and perhaps that's true, but as we walk, it's hard not to think of one of the last trips I took to West Virginia before the plague, before she died, when I was teaching creative writing in the summer program at the college in the next town over. I thought it was such a treat to come home, to talk with these eager students about my story, about how to write the complicated world of Appalachia—and the students and the faculty were so wonderful, so eager to hear my words. I thought, "This is a changed place."

One evening after a celebration dinner—it was some students' graduation—I was walking with a friend, a fellow teacher, to pick up some supplies at a nearby gas station. The friend was wearing white pants. My friend had purchased a pack of cigarettes but had neglected to buy a lighter. A man and his girlfriend were on a motorcycle at the entrance, and my friend asked the man for a light. He took one look at us, said "You're not from around here," in a way that could only be perceived as threatening. My friend was straight—tried to laugh with the man, defuse the situation, to get the light he was seeking—but my hackles had been raised. It did not matter that I was in fact from around here (though I wanted to scream that I was). The man's look and his body language were clear. We were on the cusp of violence, and I am positive that the situation would have escalated were it not for the girlfriend on the back of the bike, who, like me, could smell the acrid stench of pointless masculinity as the man on the motorcycle puffed his chest with hot air. It was the same as it always was: "Baby, shut the fuck up," or "Baby, let's get the fuck out of here," because she knew what her man was capable of and she did not want this Saturday ruined like so many others.

And so as Sam and I walk, as I recount every moment of idyll—every joyous afternoon spent running through the streets with my friends, browsing book and antique and thrift stores—I wonder if this too is not part of my mourning process, the laying to rest the world that once was, the ceding of this brick-and-block downtown to all the men on their motorcycles, the ones who look at me and Sam and men wearing white pants and see strangers, foreigners, intruders. And so as we walk, I give silent blessings to the things that helped me survive, and as I breathe in the familiar air, as I look to the man who stays close to my side, I admit to myself that everything changes and it's okay—truly okay—to let some things go, that maybe I'm not, in fact, from this place anymore, that the place I came from no longer exists.

Sam and I are finishing our walk through downtown, and I point and I point, and we sit and we recollect. What's left to do is to hop in the car and go elsewhere, to kill time until I can go to my sister's home, to see that kousa dogwood tree; but I'm not ready to let it all go—this nearly empty downtown, the sleepy streets cradled by the sleepy mountains. I can't stop hearing the way a single approaching car whirs so audibly here, how back in New York the cacophony merges to nothing. I keep finding just one more corner, one more place where my young feet pattered across the concrete, where my eyes saw something big and adult and beyond my ken. As I look out, as I run my hand over brick and block and marble and tree bark, as we walk in tightening circles, onto the old duck bridge, by the old Black school, I convince myself that we're both in these objects, she and I, a part of our souls stuck in this downtown purgatory, this place that has held my mind and my imagination since the moment I left home.

Didn't she say she loved to walk at night, back when the streets were safe, and a woman could walk without fear of a rumbling pickup truck turning the corner too fast? And didn't I, too, take to walking home after dark, except I'd be so scared because another pickup truck circled and circled and followed me and asked if I wanted a ride?

And didn't she say that she once loved a man—I remember his name—who was rich, who told her that she could have the world, who would have taken her places—the beach—but she was too scared, too young, and then our father came? Her biggest regret, she always said, and maybe mine, too (would I really have sacrificed being born if it meant she could have found happiness?).

Sam and I have walked around and around. The downtown's really so small that if I were generous I would say six blocks by six blocks. We've crisscrossed them all, and I lead him to one last stop, a square garden hidden behind a concrete wall off the side of the post office plaza. Lining the garden is a square border of stone markers, sequentially ordered, sequentially carved, in honor of each woman who served as Queen Sylvia, which is to say queen of the forest, which is to say nobody but me—and certainly not Sam—has any interest in this town festival or this town royalty or this little forgotten garden that marks the passing of time with titles and names and dates. And yet. He follows me as I trace my way back to the first stone marker—Queen Sylvia I, one Margaret Straley from Ripley, West Virginia, who was crowned in 1930, the very first Mountain State Forest Festival.

My mother used to tell the story of how she got into trouble, how there was a president who had come to town. The whole festival used to be so much bigger, she'd say, and the president—the actual president—was marching or driving through the Grand Feature Parade, with Queen Sylvia on a float close by. My mother was standing in a large crowd at the edge of the street with her friends, and as he came down the street, she made a joke about shooting him, the *him* being the president. There were Secret Service men on the roofs of the buildings, Secret Service men at his side, and one of them heard her. And then . . .

Was she questioned, was she arrested, was she pulled aside?

And this is why I'm dragging Sam through all of this, why I walk like an Alzheimer's patient on a memory walk, because it's all beginning to fade and the punch lines are gone.

When I come home I will google the Forest Festival, I will find out that five presidents attended. Franklin Roosevelt, Truman, Nixon, Ford, Carter. They were all there. But whom did she jokingly want to shoot?

I decide that you can't fact-check the dead.

I am staring at the Sylvias, and Sam asks if we're done, if we should go back to the car. He says that he's getting hungry. I say, can we just sit here for a minute and there's a granola bar in the car, and we're parked just across the street, and I won't be long.

And so we sit there, Sam and I, with the ghosts of nearly a hundred Queen Sylvias, of their patchwork dresses and their gilded crowns. We're sitting with their ghosts and the ghosts of all the others who live in spirit or memory in this town—the ghosts of my mother, of myself, of the ones who keep telling stories of long parades with presidents, with local royalty, with the tens of thousands of people lining the streets and cheering and making jokes—and we're all here in this little garden, ghosts living and dead, and though most of us will never have markers or monuments, we continue to exist nonetheless.

My sister Teresa is still busy, and we're sitting in the garden, when Katy, a friend who knows I'm in town and whom I have plans to see later, saves Sam from my memory chasing. She texts that she's heading to Pride in the Elkins City Park. It takes me a moment to put the words together. It's June 26, the same weekend as Pride back in New York. But in Elkins? I had seen a photo from a couple years back, had heard that someone in Elkins had put together an event in the park. I can remember that photo because it was so striking to me—the event looked tiny. In the photo there were a handful of lesbians sitting in lawn chairs with rainbow flags and food and not much else. Then I thought, wow, good for these strong women, fighting the tide, but also, that they looked so lonely despite their defiance.

We get up from the Queen Sylvia garden and walk a block to the rental car. Of course we'll go, I text Katy. Poor, hungry

Sam eats his granola bar in the car and I'm telling him how wild a coincidence it is that we're here in Elkins to say good-bye to my mother, to attempt to make peace with these years of fighting over me being gay, of the shame and pain that she and the town itself foisted upon me year after year, and we're going to end up at the Elkins pride event—Pride in the Park, as they call it—and we're going to celebrate openly, and for the first time that I can remember I'm not scared, I'm not worried about looking over my shoulder to see whether someone might report to my mother or my father that they saw us.

We drive the short few blocks to the park—we're just a minute or two in the car—and I'm expecting to find the lonely lesbians in their lawn chairs, a few rainbow flags, the townspeople staring with jaws agape and keeping their distance. But when we pull up to the lot at the park, we struggle to find a parking spot.

We drive to the end of the lot, wait for someone to pull out, and then we get out of the car and are greeted by what seems to be hundreds of people. I almost can't step forward. It's not the last time that day that I'll find myself so overcome that I have to stop in my tracks, hold my breath, and close my eyes to prevent myself from crying. It's such an overwhelming sight. We've spent the morning walking through my past and the memories, and the town had seemed so empty, so quiet. And yet now I find myself looking at a kind of life I never thought would exist here, not in this place, where I'd been bullied and cursed and cast aside. There are men and women and children—rainbow flags and rainbow faces and booths and lawn chairs and games and, yes, I have to squint across the grass to confirm, but there are drag queens running around. A woman approaches us and says welcome, to help ourselves to the food—she gestures to a makeshift buffet set up under a pavilion—everything is free.

There are hundreds of people (I will later read the news report to double-check, to convince myself that I wasn't exaggerating: "Several hundred people attended the third annual Pride in the Park event Saturday in the Elkins City Park"), which may not seem like a lot, but in this town of seven thousand feels incalculably large.

The first person we recognize is a man named Cody, who is someone I have met before through friends, who is one of the state representatives for the area, and only the second out gay politician in the West Virginia legislature. He gives each of us a hug, hands us a rainbow flag from his backpack. He is a politician and also a teacher at the local high school, and just after we greet him, a young woman swoops over to us—she can't be more than eighteen or nineteen—and she runs into Cody, nearly tackles him with a hug and says, "Mr. Thompson, you were my favorite teacher! I'm bisexual now!" She's so ecstatic that she seems to bounce—this self-expressed queerness so buoyant for her that she seems incapable of standing still.

There are rainbows and gay politicians and out gay children, and I'm recognizing old friends and old faces, and the narrative that I've built up about this place, about the town sinking into an ever-deeper, ever-darker abyss, begins to crack just a little. It's not that the man on the motorcycle isn't there—I see him, too, around every corner—but this is something new, something I never thought could happen.

We're mingling and chatting, and people I haven't seen in ten or twenty years are picking me out of the crowd and shouting my name and *Happy Pride*. I am barely able to keep up with the old friends, the drag queens, the politicians, the laughing and singing. I am standing under the pavilion; I'm sitting on a picnic blanket; I'm running my fingers through the grass, over the shells of acorns, of fragrant black walnuts. It's not surreal, but hyperreal, as if I've picked up a rock in the muddy grass and found an entire ecosystem, once hidden, now suddenly buzzing in the sunlight.

I'm sitting on the picnic blanket with Sam and Katy and a few other friends, and we're watching a duo of drag queens alternate on the stage. One mostly lip-synchs and dances, and in a comical moment, she steps off the stage, dances in the grass, catches her wig in a branch of a newly planted tree. The other sings in her real voice, which is good and sultry and full of Appalachian twang; she sings with gusto, as she balances on a cane, then steadies herself on the age of the stage, and points her cane at us, the Proud Marys who keep on burning. Cody, the politician, takes the stage to bless the event, to recognize himself (rightly) as only the second openly gay official elected to West Virginia's statewide government.

From the corner of my eye, I see an older man named Dub, who was once the closest thing I had to a role model at a time when I had few. He's sitting on a picnic table in the distance, with a group of women I don't know, watching the drag queens from an angle. I leave Sam and my friends and I go to him.

He's wearing his signature cowboy hat. His shirt is open to reveal the eyeball tattoo on his chest. He calls me by my last name. "Corcoran!" He pulls me into his arms.

"Phil made me promise to call him when I got here," he says, naming his partner. "He wanted to make sure that there weren't any counterprotestors, that I wouldn't get into a fistfight."

And I'll tell the story later, when my friends ask whom I was speaking to, that Dub, the son of a butcher, who grew up in a different era, was of the school that you fuck with your fuckers. As a child he'd save cow eyeballs and squish them in the face of his bullies. He was always the scariest man at any bar.

He is strong still, despite getting older. I can feel the strength in his arms as he hugs me—a firm but tender strength. You can see it in his biceps, in his cut-off shirt. I say it's unbelievable, this scene. I say I'm so happy to see him, which is more true than I can express. I can barely get out any words.

He's a talker, like so many of the people in West Virginia. I don't know how we get there, but he's segued into something about West Virginia's gay campgrounds, about the one he likes—for the redneck gays from the mountains—versus the one he doesn't like—for the DC gays who come in on the weekends. I don't really know what he's saying or why he's saying it. "I can't believe Corcoran's here!" he interjects, and taps his knee, and it's just as I remember, how he growls my surname down to nearly a single syllable. *Cork-*

"I can't believe she's been gone," I say.

And finally, "I never really got to say good-bye."

My sisters understand. They take a deep breath and I hear the same stories with slightly new embellishments. "I don't think she suffered," Teresa says. "She was so peaceful in that chair, looking up at the sky."

"She just wasn't the same after the hospital," Jackie says. "On that ride home she was so quiet."

I've heard all of this before, but this recounting of the tale in person is cleansing; their words are now part of the bath that I have been needing. *She woke up in the middle of the night and sat in the chair. She looked up at the sky, her head tilted back. She didn't suffer.*

With each iteration, with each retelling, her body becomes whole to me. For so long she has been trapped there in the purgatory of my mind. The woman who birthed me. The woman who left me. The woman who lived and suffered. I need my sisters to go on and on—and with each verb the casket of memory opens and the glimpse of her becomes a clear vision.

She woke.

She walked.

She sat.

I can see her hands crossed over her chest. And I can see her neck. And she does seem so peaceful.

She looked up.

I stand up and walk around the corner of the trailer. I am by myself for just a moment, alone there with this little pluck of a stick on the edge of Teresa's hillside; I see them, the two or three dozen leaves. This, the kousa dogwood, a thing I had never known, the thing that is now all that's left of her.

I say, "This is it?"

And Teresa says, "Yes, I put both of their ashes here."

And I look at this stub of a tree as she tells me again how she thought the tree had died, how they must have been down there fighting. That Mom must have felt bad, because it turned to spring and the tree came back to life.

And the tree came back to life.
And she came back to life.
And I see her finally.
She felt bad.
The mother I knew. Her body is fully formed. The wrinkles on her neck, the tight skin on her cheeks, her wisps of cropped, white hair. Her lips are closed. She is wearing a fine, white blouse, a simple pair of jeans. That's her, and it's just how I remember her. She's here, with me, the tree. The only time she was ever at ease was when she was sleeping.

Her eyes are closed. Her eyes are closed forever.

There is no dirt to grab, to toss.

When Sam's grandfather died we went to the swampy cemetery near the Florida coast and I wore a black yarmulke. His grandfather was buried there, next to his wife. It was just us—Sam, his mother, his father, his sister, his aunt, his uncle.

On my head is a ball cap that says "New Jersey, AP," from Asbury Park.

My sisters and their men and Sam stand around me.

She would have loved the beach at Asbury. The sand was so clean. And she would have hated it, too. All the gay men walking hand in hand.

There is only memory upon memory—so much memory that I could drown in it.

My mother died. My mother is dead.

"She's gone," I say.

Teresa says: "The doctor said it may have been an embolism. There wasn't anything we could have done."

She loved the ocean.

We turn away from the kousa dogwood tree and walk back to the picnic tables.

20

Before I knew the identity of my mother's father, I'd dreamt up a whole story of my own. It didn't make any sense and there was nothing about it that was factually true, but it became the mythology that I needed to replace the hole this man had left.

A long time ago I'd driven down I-79 toward southern West Virginia and I passed a tiny river town. I didn't even get off the exit, but from the road I could see a tight downtown crammed around a railroad depot, all the buildings and houses around the depot, along the tracks, along the river. It would be considered a nothing town these days, but it looked like it had once had a history.

I'd guess the population of the town was somewhere between five hundred and a thousand—there couldn't have been more. Something about the place—the winding river, the downtown straddling a hillside over the tracks and the river—it looked safe and even comforting. I used to play with Legos and build towns. I'd draw fantasy villages on paper. It was there, to this little town in southern West Virginia, that I went before I closed my eyes at night.

She had been a mother without a father. In my own way, so had I. I invented a curse that went back two or three hundred years. The curse was that no woman in our family would ever truly know the love of a man. The women would be abandoned, ignored. The children would be raised fatherless. This was the story of my mother. This was the story of my grandmother. It was my story, in a sense, with my own father, who himself agreed he never should have been a family man. Even my sister Teresa had found herself abandoned by the father of her child. She hadn't even given birth when he'd fled. It was a family curse. I couldn't see it any other way.

And so when I went to sleep at night, I found myself traversing the streets of that little river town. It was old-timey, and the people wore hats and overalls and high-neck dresses. They tipped their hats and curtsied as I disembarked the train.

Sometimes when I slept, I was no longer the actor in this fantasy. In my dreams, I would see her, my mother, getting off the train. It was my mother, but not the adult version of her. She was a little girl in the 1950s, seven years old, with an adult-sized valise that she could barely carry.

On the platform the locals said, "You're Patty. You've come to see the man at the lake. We'll take you there."

The taxi man came and picked up the heavy valise and put it in his trunk. He took her down a quiet road just outside of town. There was an old lakefront cabin with a tin-roofed porch, and my mother sat there with her suitcase on that porch, waiting.

The lake spread out far, maybe a mile or two, and there were trees all around the shore, and it was summer. There was an island in the middle of the lake, which divided the water and obscured the view of what lay beyond.

Suddenly, she heard the sweetest sound of a fiddle. She couldn't see where it was coming from. No one in our family had ever played music, but the smooth chords sounded like heaven to her ears. In her bones she knew this music was magical. She listened and waited in a chair on the porch of the cabin, and she looked out over the water in the late afternoon summer sun. The sounds of the fiddle seemed to come from everywhere—from the water, from the woods.

She waited and then saw the first sight of the canoe. The water was calm, and the canoe cut a gentle triangle through the reflective surface, as if it was cutting the sky and the trees. The fiddle player was there in the middle of the canoe. He played his fiddle and no one rowed. The boat seemed to move of its own accord.

He had a high brown hat, a white shirt, canvas slacks. His face was tall, vaguely like Abraham Lincoln, and his cheekbones were high and rigid, just like my mother's.

And she saw then the most curious sight—swans, eight of them, following in the wake of the boat.

He played a tune that never seemed to stop—one that was old but familiar—until he reached the shore just in front of the porch.

"My daughter," he said, and she recognized him as the man from the railroad tracks who threw pennies.

"I knew you'd come one day."

He gestured with a tap of his fiddle bow against the canoe. "Get in."

The boat took off again toward the island in the middle of the lake, and he set to playing that same song. She would never play the fiddle or learn to read music, but those notes would be pressed to the walls of her heart.

"I have a gift," he said, and with a tilt of his head, she saw the swans. "They'll follow me wherever I go."

And he played and the boat floated inward and the swans followed.

"We're cursed, you know," he said.

And she just nodded her head.

"You'll never see me again except once when I will come to check up on you," he said. "Then you won't recognize me. In fact, you'll have forgotten that we ever met. That too is part of the curse. But when you see me, you'll know from the deepest place inside of you that I am your father, come to make sure you are alive and well."

He played and played as the sun began to set over the western edge of the lake, over the forest. He stopped one more time.

"The curse does not have to be forever," he said. "One day a woman in your family will give birth to a boy. It could be you. He won't be like other boys. He will be a child with a gentle heart. Too gentle at times. You will love him more than anything, but he'll break you into many pieces."

Again, she nodded.

"To break the curse, it will be you who will abandon him."

And after he spoke that last sentence, another canoe came out from under the tree and floated over to where they were. She instinctively stepped from her father's boat into this empty one. It whisked her back to the shore, and her father disappeared behind the island.

He did not say that he loved her. It was understood that this too was part of the curse.

At the lake house, the taxi man was waiting for her. He picked up her valise. He took her back through the little town she now understood was her heritage.

When she boarded the train to head back home to her mother and her wicked stepfather, she knew—even though she was only seven years old—that she would be the one, the woman who would give birth to a boy that would be at times too much like a woman, a boy whom she would love more than herself, a boy that would tear the flesh from her body time and time again. But this was the way it must be.

I once received a message from one of my mother's childhood friends. She had found me on social media. Her name was Gretchen, and she wrote to me the year before my father died.

She said she lived in Elkins "about 1,000 years ago." Despite this, she said, "I still look amazing." She said she'd grown up on the same street as my mother, that they'd passed their time lying and covering up for each other.

"We weren't bad," she said. "We just had to hide Patty from her crazy family. It doesn't sound like much has changed."

It was the start of a brief correspondence. She told me little stories about their shared past, about their life running around in their neighborhood. She sometimes turned to the subject of me. She said, "I remember holding you when you were just a month or so old. You were so perfect, and absolutely beautiful."

Our conversations remained mostly one-sided; I wasn't talking to my mother then, and I didn't know if I had the energy to explain the decade of our fighting. I never knew what my mother told her friends about our relationship.

Gretchen's words vacillated from playful and quirky to serious and concerned. She said, "I love your Mom so much and I'm so glad she has you for a son. You put a smile as big as Christmas on her face when she mentions you. It makes me happy to see Patty with a family she deserves. She never had one until now. I'm sorry but I won't include Jack. He never helped your mom with anything for you kids. She has made sacrifices all her life for her kids and let herself go."

Gretchen lived in Pittsburgh, and she told me that she wanted so desperately to take my mother away from my father and bring her there. She'd in fact offered to do just that, but my mother had apparently refused. My mother told her she couldn't leave him.

She would rattle on and on about things that I had only loosely known, and I'd take it all in. She'd catch herself—notice that I wasn't responding—and then she'd take a break for a week or two. She seemed to understand, without my saying, that I needed a little room to process what I was hearing—this new perspective on my mother's life. She'd afforded me this grace even from her first message. She'd written, "Well kiddo, I've gone on like we're the best of friends and I know you won't remember me."

She was right. I didn't remember her. But there was something about what she'd said—the honesty, the frankness—I don't think any of her friends had been so straight with me. I don't think any of her friends had ever spoken openly to me about her "crazy family" or about my father, who "never helped" anyone in his family. And importantly, even if I didn't admit it at the time, her words were another window—another confirmation—that even when we were apart, even during the deepest of our silences, my mother cared for me deeply.

A smile as big as Christmas, she'd said.

We were in touch for a few months, and then the messages went silent. When I searched for her profile on social media, I found out that she had passed away. There was so much I had wanted to ask her.

On the day I visited the kousa dogwood tree in June of 2021, a year and nearly three months after my mother died, I told my sisters

I was writing this book. I told them that I had tried to write this book many times over the course of my life, but that I didn't want to hurt her, that I didn't want to hurt her while she was still alive. Teresa, who has never really criticized my choices, said she thought it was best to leave dead bodies in the ground. She did not press the subject further.

I understand her concern. When she talks about my mother, she sees an angel in heaven with my father. When Jackie talks about my mother, she talks about how lonely it has become during the holidays. They remember the good times, the fond memories, the life that my mother lived largely outside of my purview.

When I think back to being a kid, as far back as I can go, I see them both there. Teresa taking me out to the park, lying to strangers, telling them that I was her own child; Jackie grabbing me by the hand, rushing me out the front door to find a moment of peace. They protected me from the worst of it—the fighting, the near-violence. We're all still in touch, but it's hard for us to go back to those old places. I wonder about the depth of their scars.

I think about the version of my mother that my sisters knew, and I think about the version they choose to hold onto. I've seen the photos and the videos that they share—on the first birthday after her death, on Christmas, on New Year's Eve. There is my mother drunk at a bar, nearly falling over with laughter! There she is in the beautiful dress, the playful hat, the perfect makeup. There are her old best friends reminiscing on social media about the times they had, how they tore up the town. I was the baby of the family. I remind myself again that by the time I left the house for college, she had been raising children for thirty-two years straight—an amount of time that correlates roughly with the total of my conscious memory.

My sisters see my mother as beautiful as she always was, smiling with the light of God in her eyes. I am glad that she has someone to remember her like that.

Acknowledgments

A version of this book has been in the works since I was twenty years old, so my gratitude extends the distance between that sometimes vivid past and now. First are the writers and teachers. I began toying with these words in a creative nonfiction class, where Carol DeBoer-Langworthy guided us through the process of a thing called Lifewriting. I still think of you, Jayne Anne, when I was sitting in your office as a new graduate student and you said to me, "I want to hear that story." Tayari, you're a superstar writer and still find the time to encourage everyone around you; with your kindness, you've made me feel like an actual writer. Carter, your feedback on and belief in this book made me ready to share it with the world. I want to thank Mesha and Matt, a power duo who offer friendship and editorial guidance in equal doses. Leora, you popped up again in my life just as I was wrapping up these words—you were there at the beginning and the end. I shared an early draft of an early chapter with my favorite writing group: thank you, Ian and Max, for those first looks. Roberto—your poetry keeps my own words grounded in the lyric. I am so grateful for Abby, my editor and biggest supporter, who made sure this story would find a home.

This book was written because I was loved and cared for by so many, starting with Sara and Emily, and then Morgan and Mandy. Thanks to my loves Britt and Krissy. To Lauren, who let me use our shared story of grief. And the moms—all the moms! I wrote much of this with the fresh memory of my beloved Gerry, who took me

235

in that first Christmas and who would have loved this book. I will always remember my childhood with Helen and the witches. Lynne and Harvey, I could never thank you enough, for treating me with dignity, like I was your own son. I want to thank my sisters, who lived through much of this, who were often my protectors.

I will never stop thinking about my mother.

Finally, I have to thank my love and partner through all of this. Sam, I am so happy that you stuck with me that day, that you were there to pick me up off the cold Maine ground.

About the Author

Jonathan Corcoran is the author of the story collection *The Rope Swing*, which was a finalist for the Lambda Literary Awards and long-listed for the Story Prize. His essays and stories have been published and anthologized widely, including in *Eyes Glowing at the Edge of the Woods: Fiction and Poetry from West Virginia* and *Best Gay Stories*. He received a BA in Literary Arts from Brown University and an MFA in Fiction Writing from Rutgers University–Newark. Jonathan teaches writing at New York University. He was born and raised in a small town in West Virginia and currently resides in Brooklyn, New York. Learn more at jonathancorcoranwrites.com.

Appalachian Futures

BLACK, NATIVE, AND QUEER VOICES

Series editors

Annette Saunooke Clapsaddle, Davis Shoulders,
and Crystal Wilkinson

A book series that gives voice to Black, Native, Latinx, Asian, Queer, and other nonwhite or ignored identities within the Appalachian region.